How to Conduct a Formative Evaluation

Barry K. Beyer

D1608026

Association for Supervision and Curriculum Development
Alexandria, Virginia

The Author
Barry K. Beyer is Professor Emeritus of the Graduate School of Education,
George Mason University, Fairfax, VA 22030.

Association for Supervision and Curriculum Development
1250 N. Pitt Street • Alexandria, VA 22314
Telephone: (703) 549-9110 • Fax: (703) 549-3891

Printed in the United States of America.

Gene R. Carter, *Executive Director*
Ronald S. Brandt, *Director of Publications*
Nancy Modrak, *Managing Editor, ASCD Books*
Carolyn R. Pool, *Associate Editor*
Gary Bloom, *Manager, Design and Production Services*
Stephanie A. Justen, *Print Production Coordinator*
Valerie Sprague, *Desktop Publisher*

From the Editors: We welcome readers' comments on ASCD books
and other publications. If you would like to give us your opinion of
this book or suggest topics for future books, please write to ASCD,
Managing Editor of Books, 1250 N. Pitt St., Alexandria, VA 22314.

ASCD Stock No. 1-95183
ISBN: 0-87120-244-1

Library of Congress Cataloging-in-Publication Data

Beyer, Barry K., 1931-
   How to conduct a formative evaluation / Barry K. Beyer.
     p. cm.
   ISBN 0-87120-244-1
   1. Educational evaluation—United States. 2. Instructional
systems—Design—United States—Evaluation. I. Title.
LB2822.75.B45 1995
379.1'54'0973—dc20
                                      95-4411
                                      CIP

How to Conduct a Formative Evaluation

Introduction:
How Do We Know It
Will Work?

How do we know it will work? This is probably the most
frequently asked question about educational innovations,
reforms, and other products. The developers of the
programs ask it. Funding agencies, sponsors, regulatory
agencies, boards of education, administrators, teachers,
and even parents and students ask it. People ask this
question over and over again whenever anyone proposes or
requests funds to develop a curriculum or instructional
innovation of consequence. And the question is not an idle
one. The answers will reveal both the quality of the
proposed product and the effort spent in its development.

Of course, we cannot predict exactly and with
confidence how an idea will work in practice. In developing
an innovative program or product, we may have good
reason to *believe* that our innovation will work as
intended—or at least *should* work—but we don't know,
beyond a reasonable doubt, whether it actually will work.
Yet unless we can assure people that a new product stands
a reasonable chance of performing as desired, or planned,
or claimed, few sponsors or gatekeepers are likely to
endorse it or invest in producing it. How *do* we know it will
work?

In the field of curriculum and instructional
development, *formative evaluation can answer this question.*
Formative evaluation consists of assessing educational
programs or other kinds of educational products *while* they
are being developed, to help shape them into their final
forms. I believe it is the key to successfully developing any
educational product. If we don't use a thorough formative

1

evaluation, the educational product developed isn't likely to work well in practice. This applies to all sorts of curriculum development—whether an elementary or secondary school course or curriculum; a university degree program; a textbook, computer software, site-based management, or other kinds of instructional or learning material; or any other type of educational innovation, reform, or change.

Whatever evaluative feedback we generate—and use—while developing a new product determines the quality of that product. Feedback may be repeated in loops—development, feedback, more development, field testing, changes to the product, and so forth. These development efforts should include a well-designed and executed formative evaluation based on sound research, theory, and exemplary practice. This process will either allow for termination after only a minimum of invested funds and effort if the proposed product fails to make the grade—or will produce a product that will work as intended. A new curriculum program will work if we carry out a continuing formative assessment and use what we find out to modify or refine the program en route to producing it in its final form.

Despite the importance of formative evaluation in curriculum and instructional development, however, it is one of the least-well-done parts of such development. Some of the reasons for its neglect are inadequate funding, poor timing, little interest, and inadequate staff. The most significant reason for the low priority given to formative evaluation in most development efforts, however, is that many sponsors and developers do not understand what formative evaluation is. Many people do not understand the crucial role it plays in development—and how it can be done and done well. Too few of us seem to be as familiar as we should be with the appropriate procedures, tools, and questions to employ along the way. This book addresses this gap.

How to Conduct a Formative Evaluation is intended for those whose job it is to develop new educational programs and products or evaluate such products as they are being developed. It also applies to those who oversee or sponsor such efforts. It seeks to make the design and conduct of formative evaluation easier, more thorough, and more complete, and as a result to ensure the quality of the final products developed for use in our schools. It is the product of years of experience as well as of theory and research.

During my 37 years as a professional educator, I have developed or codeveloped many educational programs and instructional materials. Among them are elementary and secondary school lessons, units, courses, and curriculums; university courses and programs, doctoral programs included; and training programs. I helped develop instructional and learning materials, including transparencies, filmstrips, something called inquiry maps, and with a superb team of colleagues, a major best-selling textbook series. Formative evaluation played a role in developing all, although it was more significant in some than in others. Unfortunately, when I first started in the business of development in the late 1950s, there were few, if any, places to go for practical assistance in how to conduct an appropriate formative evaluation. As nearly as I can determine, there still aren't many. Thus, this guide.

I have prepared this book as much out of frustration as out of a desire to make life easier for anyone facing the challenges of planning or conducting a formative evaluation. My frustration arose, as you may have guessed, from being unable to find in one source a complete presentation of what is now known about conducting a good formative evaluation, coupled with my awareness that such information does exist, even if scattered in bits and pieces throughout our professional literature. My desire to help others to do a better job at formative evaluation arose out of my arriving at a deep sense of the crucial role that formative evaluation plays in successful curriculum and instructional development. Newly developed products would benefit if developers could only become better informed about this important part of the educational development process *before* they get involved in doing it—or in trying to do it.

This book thus pulls together information about formative evaluation from two major sources, supplemented and mediated by my own experience in this field. Some information about formative evaluation, produced by scholars and specialists in educational evaluation and development, can be found scattered throughout various scholarly journals and books. In addition, participants in exemplary development efforts have also generated valuable information about formative evaluation and its practical applications, much of which lies embedded in hard-to-find reports and case studies of their development efforts. Most students and practitioners of curricular and instructional development have neither the time nor the resources to locate this information and put it into useful form, so I have tried to do that here.

I have also tried to keep this guide brief and practical. I believe that anyone charged with the responsibility of learning about or conducting curriculum or instructional development will find such a presentation useful. I hope these contents will help those of us engaged in this task to design and conduct formative evaluations that provide feedback most useful in producing top-quality educational products and eliminate the necessity of having to discover on the job, often too late, how such evaluations can best be (or should have been) done. To that end, this book incorporates the best of what both experts and practitioners in the field know about this important task.

* * *

Appropriately, this guide has gone through its own formative evaluation as it has progressed through its development. It has been reviewed by experts in educational program and instructional development, by practitioners in the field, and by potential developers and evaluators. And it has been used, in draft form, to design formative evaluations of various types of educational products, from courses of study to new kinds of teaching materials. As presented here, this guide incorporates modifications and revisions based on the feedback generated by these formative trials and assessments. I wish to acknowledge here especially the feedback and suggestions given me as a result of this evaluation by Mary Anne Lecos, formerly Assistant Superintendent for Instructional Services of the Fairfax County, Virginia, Public Schools, and by her present George Mason University colleagues, Professors Evelyn Jacob, Jack Levy, and Linda

Seligman, as well as by University of Washington Professor Walter Parker and George Mason University doctoral students and experienced educators, particularly Cathy Wilson and David Checcino. In developing this guide, I have tried to practice what it teaches.

BARRY K. BEYER
Fairfax, Virginia

1
Formative Evaluation: Its Nature and Importance

OF ALL PARTS OF THE PROCESS OF DEVELOPING PRODUCTS FOR USE IN education, none seems to be more neglected or abused than formative evaluation. We develop many programs and products—curriculums, individual courses of study, textbooks, computer software, videos, or instructional methodologies—but we often don't evaluate them well before they reach their final form. Whether we just don't understand formative evaluation, or say we don't have time or money to do it, formative evaluation of educational products seems to be either grossly inadequate or missing altogether in most curriculum and instructional development efforts. This is true not only of school-based efforts, but of commercial development efforts, as well. It is also true at the precollege, college, and university levels. And it is true of efforts managed by professional educators, as well as by trainers in business and industry. Formative evaluation is usually the last part of the process to be planned (if included at all) or the first cut or eliminated when time or money appears to be in short supply.

Yet formative evaluation is critical to the process of developing any new curriculum, teaching strategies, or instructional materials. Without formative evaluation, such products are unlikely to meet the standards of their developers or the needs of their intended users as well as they could or should. Knowing how to conduct an effective formative evaluation—and doing so—distinguishes a quality educational development effort from an unacceptable one, just as it distinguishes a potentially useful educational product from a potentially useless one.

The Nature of Formative Evaluation

Formative evaluation, simply put, means evaluating or assessing a product *while* that product is in the process of being created and shaped. Formative evaluation serves development rather than implementation purposes.[1] *The primary goal of formative evaluation is to improve the quality of the product being developed so that it will be as likely as possible in everyday use to achieve the objectives it was designed for.* Product revision takes place in light of the information generated by the evaluation and before the product takes final form.

Formative evaluation is distinguished by three features:

- It is ongoing.
- It involves assessment.
- It seeks specific information as well as judgments.

Formative evaluation *is ongoing* in that it occurs repeatedly, at various stages throughout the development process, from the design or platform stage through the prototype (draft), pilot, and field trial stages of the product.

It *involves assessment,* making informed judgments focusing on how well the product, at whatever stage of development it is in when being assessed, meets criteria indicating the extent to which it is likely to produce the results intended.

Finally, because the information secured from each formative assessment is to be used to restructure or otherwise modify the product, formative evaluation *seeks specific information* as well as judgments or opinions. Those judgments and information together serve as feedback for product improvement rather than for purposes of "grading."

---

[1]Formative evaluation can be applied to the process of product development, as well as to student learning or achievement-in-progress. While many of the principles and procedures presented here can be used for formative evaluation in these other areas, the focus here is strictly on formative evaluation in the development of educational curriculums, courses, instructional materials, and teaching strategies.

Thus, formative evaluation is exactly what its name asserts. It is formative. Its results are intended to shape or *form* the content, structure, or other features of a product being developed. Formative evaluation is the primary way an idea or intent or plan becomes a product that has a high potential for producing or achieving its predetermined objectives. In the absence of such evaluation, no educational product is likely to achieve its intended quality.

Formative evaluation is *not* the same as summative evaluation. These two types of evaluation occur at different points in the development process and serve markedly different purposes (Scriven 1967, Borg and Gall 1989). Summative evaluation of an educational product occurs *after* a product has been completely developed and is in use or ready for use on a large scale. Such evaluation seeks to determine the value of a given product for a given clientele and is most often used in making decisions about purchasing, adopting, implementing, or continuing a specific educational product. Summative evaluation, in essence, helps us decide what to do with an educational product that already exists.

Formative evaluation, on the other hand, assists in the creation of a new product. Since it occurs *during* development, the results of formative evaluation are used to improve or shape a product before it is fully developed, distributed, or put into general use. Without formative evaluation, educational product development would indeed be risky and, perhaps, not an especially productive business.

The Importance of Formative Evaluation

Why is formative evaluation such an important part of curriculum or instructional development?

First, formative evaluation is the most practical, cost-effective way of determining the quality—or potential quality—of a newly developed product before it is put into regular use. Obviously, the best way to determine how well a product will do what it is supposed to do when "used as directed" is to use it when, where, and how it is supposed to be used and then to determine whether or not the outcome matches the stated objectives or the intended results. To make such a determination, however, we must wait until the product has been fully developed. If this were the way developers evaluated their products, it would be comparable to producing a new medicine (such as Thalidomide or Fialuridine, for example) and then giving it to large numbers of users without any prior efforts to see if it really works as intended or has any negative or other unanticipated consequences.

Such an approach to developing virtually anything would be both unwise and impractical. It would be unwise because there is always the possibility that the product in question will not work as intended or will produce adverse consequences, with irreparable damage to its initial users. It would be impractical because if a hitherto unevaluated product, when it is finally put into full-scale use, turns out to be a failure or less than desired or acceptable in terms of quality or performance, the efforts and resources that went into its development and production would have been wasted. Waiting for the final product to find out if it will work as intended is simply unacceptable to potential users, developers, and funders.

Formative evaluation is important for another reason, too. As developers, we are often so close to our products and so limited in our expertise that we frequently lack the inclination to examine our work in a way that will detect inadequacies and identify opportunities for improvement. Sometimes we are unaware of our own biases or of the limitations of our particular points of view or experiences. Sometimes we are too far removed in time and experience from the ultimate users of the products and thus are unfamiliar with what is meaningful and of interest to them. And many of us are too discipline bound or content oriented to understand the nuances of process-in-learning—or focus so much on process and procedure that we may be poorly informed about the content and substance of the product being developed.

Formative evaluation addresses these conditions in a constructive way. By submitting successive drafts or models of our proposed creations to the examination of experts, representative potential users, and other interested parties, we can avoid errors arising from unrecognized bias, faulty assumptions, and erroneous or outdated information or data. By recycling the feedback obtained into revised iterations of the product, we can ultimately produce a product that will work as intended without ill effects or other unwelcome surprises for its intended users.

Common Problems with Formative Evaluation

Despite its importance, however, formative evaluation frequently is poorly carried out in the development of educational products. Too many of us treat it as a formality at best, or as an obstacle or nuisance at worst, and make little serious effort to conduct a useful evaluation. Instead, we often enlist superiors or friends to review the product and ask questions such as, "What do you think of the tone and language of the material?" Or we ask prospective users or so-called experts their opinions about whether, on a scale of 1 to 5, future users might enjoy it. Questions like these are so broad and imprecise they fail to pinpoint specific places in the product where changes, if needed, can be made; responses to such questions are of little use in product improvement.

Occasionally, some developers even conduct pre- and post-objective test assessments of the first trial of the product without properly training the individual(s) using it, erroneously expecting first-time users to be skilled enough in their use of the product to use it flawlessly and as designed. And some of us even try out or use a newly developed product with a group of users out of the sequence or the context for which it was designed. These assessments engage users without the prerequisite skills, knowledge, or other background experience required to use the product successfully or to full advantage. Such efforts at formative evaluation are shams, at best. They seriously undermine the quality of both the development effort and the product resulting from that effort.

Formative evaluation, as we usually see it practiced, suffers from six critical flaws:

• *Using unqualified people as expert evaluators.* There is more to expertise than longevity in a field or a title. Not all school principals or supervisors or college professors or teachers may be experts in instruction. Not all teachers with master's degrees or with 10 or more years of experience may be expert in the body of content they teach. Yet time after time, people are proposed and used as evaluators solely on the basis of years of experience, rank, or title.

• *Failing to give specific or appropriate guidance to evaluators on what to look for.* Many people enlisted to provide formative evaluation and feedback in a development effort are inexperienced in this task and do not know the kinds of information most useful to developers—or what we really want or need to know. For example, whereas we need to know early on about the structure and workability of an educational product we're developing, first-time evaluators left on their own usually focus on more obvious product features such as spelling or how objectives are stated. Although it is essential early on to identify gaps, irrelevancies, or redundancies in content and practice, few evaluators provide such information on their own initiative.

• *Asking for general opinions or judgments without defining criteria or relating the requested responses to specific segments of the product being evaluated.* Questionnaires that ask, "Did your students enjoy this lesson or this material?" provide little, if any, useful information because such questions do not pinpoint anything specific that we can alter or capitalize on. Evaluators need specific, rather than general, directions to follow, criteria to use, questions to answer, and tasks to do. In many cases, their initial comments or responses may even then require follow-up interviews for clarification.

• *Failing to seek the kinds of information most useful in improving the quality of a product.* In constructing a new educational product, we need feedback on the accuracy, structure, and clarity of the content and the structure and workability of suggested learning strategies—not simply whether the product is enjoyable, motivating, generally accurate, or relevant. We must explicitly seek specific kinds of information during the formative evaluation process if we expect to produce a worthwhile product.

• *Failing to continuously assess an educational product throughout the entire course of its development.* Each iteration (draft) or reiteration (redraft) of an educational product should be assessed. An assessment done only at an early stage of development cannot account for the impact of alterations or revisions made between that time and the production of the final version of the product. We cannot assume that a change made as a result of earlier formative feedback resolves the problem it was intended to resolve (or does not cause an unanticipated problem) without evaluating the change in practice. Assessing changes as they are made can prevent revisions from having unexpected or negative impacts further down the line and can ensure progress toward the production of a quality product.

• *Failing to allow enough time for the evaluation and constructive use of its results.* It takes time to conduct a formative evaluation—from 2 to 4 weeks to secure expert reviews or critiques to a semester or a year to secure large-scale evaluation of a new course of study. It takes additional time before that to design, evaluate, and revise the evaluation instruments and procedures to be used—and even more time to analyze the data secured by the evaluation and make appropriate alterations or revisions in the draft product. Rushing through or cutting time from any phase of formative evaluation simply compromises the ultimate quality of the product. When done well, formative evaluation always seems to take more time than allowed or expected.

If we are committed to producing the best products possible, we should make serious efforts to avoid these problems by carefully planning and conducting well-thought-out formative evaluations throughout the entire development process. The next chapter discusses when to conduct a formative evaluation and how to design its structure.

2
When to Conduct Formative Evaluations and What to Look For

WHEN WE PLAN AND CARRY OUT A FORMATIVE EVALUATION OF ANY educational product or program we are developing, we must remember that the purpose of the assessment is to produce a better product. Therefore, we must plan and conduct an evaluation that secures the kinds of information that we can plow back into our development effort to improve our product. To do this, we can respond to four major questions:

- When are the best times or points in the development process to secure formative feedback?
- What do we need to find out as we move this product through each major point in the development process to be sure the product, in final form, will accomplish what it is designed to accomplish?
- Who, what, and where are the best sources of this information?
- How best can we secure this information in the detail and degree of specificity we need to make appropriate changes and improvements as development proceeds?

Figure 2.1 presents these questions (in shortened form) in a matrix that shows their relationships to each other. By answering each question in terms of each point in the development process when formative evaluation will yield the most benefits, we can fashion the best possible education products. This chapter provides information relevant to each of these questions. It concludes with suggestions on how to use an elaboration of this matrix to incorporate the ideas and guidelines presented into coherent, purposeful formative evaluations for any educational product.

FIGURE 2.1

Key Questions in Planning Formative Evaluation

What are the key evaluation points?	What do we need to find out?	Who evaluates?	How can we secure this information?
1.			
2.			
3.			
4.			

From Barry K. Beyer, *How to Conduct a Formative Evaluation* (Alexandria, Va.: Association for Supervision and Curriculum Development, 1995). Copyright © 1995 by Barry K. Beyer. Charts and figures may be reproduced for educational purposes only.

When to Conduct Formative Evaluations

Most educational development efforts go through clearly identifiable stages (Grobman 1970, Schaffarzick and Hampson 1975, Borg and Gall 1989, Pratt 1980). Formative evaluation can—and should—occur during at least four of these stages in the development process: design, prototype, pilot, and field test.

Design

The design stage usually produces a document that describes the product or program to be developed. The document presents the general goal of the product, its major objectives, its primary intended audience, and its essential components and how they relate to each other. It often identifies the assumptions on which the product will be based and describes potential users. This design also identifies the learning and teaching or other principles the product will be constructed on, the main elements of the content to be included, the structure of the proposed product, and the operating specifications the final product will be expected to meet (or its final uses). This information serves, in effect, as a launching *platform* for the development effort and as the *blueprint* for what is to be developed. The appropriate formative evaluation at this point in the process is to circulate this document to experts for evaluative feedback, including challenges to the basic principles and assumptions underlying the proposed design.

Prototype

The next stage, the prototype, produces a model or draft (sample chapter, lesson plans, sequence of frames or learning activities, assessment devices, or activities) of each essential, new, or unique component of the product. A prototype is a mockup—not necessarily full scale and certainly not in final full color or polished form—of the product under development. For computer software, the prototype may be a storyboard of screens; in an instructional guide, it may be a complete lesson plan or module just as users will see it; in a text, it may be a draft of a complete chapter showing all the features to be included.

Not all educational product development efforts may lend themselves to producing a prototype of the complete product or of one or more of its components. If we develop such a model, however, formative evaluation at this point usually consists of asking several people to work through it or read it (if a draft of written material) to estimate how well it actually works as intended and is feasible.

Developers themselves often conduct or directly observe these tryouts because they know what the particular prototype is intended to accomplish and how it is supposed to work. Consequently, they are the most likely to use the product as it was originally intended to be used. Their intimate knowledge of the product sometimes allows them to find errors, determine when there is a problem, and identify solutions or even create alternatives or modifications right on the spot. In fact, it is not uncommon for one developer to actively conduct the tryout of a prototype while one or more codevelopers closely observe and monitor the process (Gagne and Briggs 1974, Dick and Carey 1985).

In some instances, we can combine the pilot stage, discussed next, with this prototype stage. We might consider even replacing the prototype with a pilot if the product contains no unusual or innovative components, such as new instructional or learning strategies or activities, materials, or tasks. However, when we include a new or unusual component, we should try out a prototype of the component by itself and revise it as necessary before incorporating it into the larger prototype or pilot. Thus, a prototype of a new structure for learning would normally be tried out, evaluated, and revised at this stage before being incorporated into a first draft of a complete product, which then could be piloted in full.

Pilot

At the pilot stage, a complete version of each component of the product or program is prepared for use. Although it may not be in final, polished form, the product is usable with no explanatory intervention from the developers. We can often use a formative evaluation at this point to identify user reactions, as well as to elicit any ideas that might add to or improve the quality of the product. To secure the most useful feedback, we should ensure that several experts examine the product. We should also see that a small but representative sample of intended users actually use the product under controlled conditions to determine if it will work as intended.

A new kind of instructional material, type of lesson, or manual should be used by two or three representative target users, closely monitored by a trained observer. A curriculum guide should be examined and put into operation by several people with a small number of students representative of those who will use it in larger numbers later. At the pilot stage, as in testing or trying out a prototype, the developer may conduct the trial of the pilot form of the product or directly observe its use. Components of the product may not be tried out in sequence at this stage or even tried by the same evaluators, unless sequence is critical to their effective use. We may wish to repeat the pilot stage several times, if we make significant revisions in or additions to the product as a result of the pilot testing.

Field Test

The next stage, field testing, consists of trying out all the components of a newly developed product in their intended sequence by a large, representative sample of users in the real-world context where the final product is expected to be used. At this point, we will have developed a complete version of the product or program, debugged it as much as possible through prior formative evaluations, and ensured that it is ready for formal use on a large scale without our own intervention.

Field trials vary in number and scale. Often, two field trials occur. The first generally involves a significant but limited number of representative users, perhaps 50 to 100 or so, if the product is a course or piece of instructional material such as a textbook or computer software. The second field trial usually involves 2 to 10 times that number of users and occurs after revisions have been made as a result of the smaller preceding field trial. Formative evaluation in the field trial stage focuses on the following:

• How workable the product is for typical users in a real-world setting

• How well the product accomplishes the objectives for which it was designed

Developers normally do not intervene in the use of the product during these trials. At this stage of development, however, we must ensure that the product is used exactly as designed. As development specialist Walter Borg has noted, we cannot assume that people directed or even trained to use educational products a specific way will do so automatically on their own. Yet, unless they do so at this stage of the development process, the results of field trial evaluations will be suspect, to say the least (Borg 1987).

Formative evaluation involves serious and continuing efforts at each stage of product development to find out what is working or not working—or would work better—in the product under development.[2] At each stage, evaluation should deal with all the components of the product—for an instructional product, with student learning materials, content, instructional and learning activities and procedures, and instructors' manuals; for a curriculum, with the objectives, content, learning activities, learning materials, assessment procedures, supplemental materials, and rationale; or for educational software, with the program, student materials, and instructor guide.

The development of educational products is a series of recursive cycles of continuing design, tryout, evaluation, and revision and redesign, retryout, reevaluation, and so on. Formative evaluation is the key to this entire process. During such evaluation at each stage of development, errors or problems become apparent; new, unanticipated options become evident; and hidden assumptions become explicit and perhaps candidates for alteration. Formative evaluation permits us to better mesh our ideas with reality in trying to accomplish our development objectives. Without it, the quality of newly developed products would be questionable, indeed.

What We Need to Find Out Through Formative Evaluation ____

What do we need to learn during the process of development to ensure the quality of our products? According to experts in educational development, we need to elicit from qualified evaluators information that will indicate how well our proposed product is likely to work and how well it will ultimately work to accomplish its intended objectives (e.g., Baker 1973, Borg and Gall 1989, Dick and Carey 1985). For products such as curriculums, programs, instructional or learning materials, tests, and manuals, we need information about the following:

---

[2]In a sense, formative evaluation never ends. Once a product is adopted for large-scale use, its users can provide feedback for updating or further revising it. Many users actually alter a product as they use it, sometimes in an effort to fill in gaps or accommodate changes not completely anticipated by the developers. However, this continuing "formative" revision is more *re*-formative and occurs after the initial development effort concludes. Therefore, it is not included here as part of the formative process of product development.

- Gaps in the content of the product
- Irrelevancies in the content
- Sufficiency of the content, examples, and practices for mastery or understanding
- Accuracy of the content
- Clarity of the information, directions, and tasks
- Workability of any activities or tasks included, given the ability, experience, and knowledge levels of the intended users and the time available
- How well the structure and sequence of the material enables its users to achieve the stated objectives and to develop an appropriate level of understanding
- Unanticipated or unintended consequences or outcomes of the product—negative as well as positive
- Congruence between product objectives, identified user needs, learning material or content, learning activities or using procedures, and learner assessment
- User-friendliness of the product, in terms of potential users' presumed or diagnosed entry-level skills, knowledge, experiences, interests, abilities, and concerns

These areas are generic concerns for all educational development efforts. We may find, however, that we need other kinds of information more specific to the type of product being developed. For example, reading or developmental level or types of practice provided may be especially relevant when we are developing a mathematics text or computer software.

As important as the generic types of information are, they are not emphasized equally throughout the process. The kinds of information we solicit, as well as the kinds of evaluators, data-gathering procedures, and instruments used, differ at each stage of the development process. For example, we need to deal with concerns about gaps, irrelevancies, accuracy, and sufficiency in the early stages of development, well before a field trial. At the prototype and pilot stages, we will need to address workability in terms of time allocation, user-friendliness, and clarity of directions. And we certainly should resolve issues or concerns about these features before the field trials. How well a product achieves the product objectives, on the other hand, is a major focus of evaluation at the field trial stage rather than at earlier evaluation points. How well we build in opportunities to gather and use appropriate information throughout the development process of all components of the intended product is a key measure of the quality of our effort and a key indicator of whether the product is likely to succeed.

3
Sources of Formative Feedback

AS WE DEVELOP NEW EDUCATIONAL PRODUCTS, PROGRAMS, OR OTHER innovations, we can secure formative feedback from many sources. Identifying and arranging to use these sources should occur early in the development cycle. The most useful sources are of two kinds:

• People who can provide evaluative feedback about the product under development

• Well-established standards that developers can refer to in the process of development

Types of Evaluators

Assistance from at least three types of people is essential in the formative evaluation of any educational product: experts, users, and "stakeholders."

Experts

Four kinds of experts customarily can contribute: experts in content or subject matter; experts in cognition, skill development, or in other processes (such as communication or programming) involved in the product; experts in the delivery of the product; and people especially knowledgeable about the intended users of the product, their skill levels, existing knowledge, interests, concerns, and other relevant attributes. For example, formative evaluation of an elementary school social studies curriculum would benefit immensely from evaluation by experts in the various disciplines that make up this field (geography, history, political science, and so on). Other evaluators might be experts in instructional design, in elementary school curriculum and instruction, and in the nature and development of elementary school youngsters.

Users

Two kinds of users—primary and secondary—can also provide useful formative feedback. Primary users are those who will use the product to achieve the product's specified objectives—learners and instructors in the case of instructional materials such as textbooks and computer learning programs, or administrators in the case of manuals on how to carry out some administrative task, or teachers in the case of a curriculum guide or teaching manual.

Secondary users are those affected by how the primary users use the product—for example, employers, college instructors, and parents in the case of students who use newly developed instructional materials or programs; or teachers, students, and others who are affected by how an administrator employs what is learned in a newly developed administrative manual. Many people could be involved in the formative evaluation of any educational product.

We ought to be sure that users—especially primary users—have varying degrees of experience and abilities. *Novice* users are those who have never before used the product or anything like it, and *experienced* users have used similar products in the past or have already experienced what the product proposes to offer. Both can provide useful feedback for formative purposes about virtually any educational product.

Both novice and experienced users of a program or product can identify gaps and irrelevancies in materials or procedures, lack of clarity in directions, task difficulties or appropriateness, and adequacy of practice opportunities. Experienced users can also suggest alternative approaches, tasks, directions, content, and examples. Some of these suggestions may work better or be more relevant to users than those included in a first draft of a proposed product.

Likewise, novice users with varying ability levels can provide differing and valuable formative feedback (Dick and Carey 1985). Novices of below-average ability or unique backgrounds can provide useful feedback about clarity and sequence of directions and tasks, as well as the appropriateness and meaningfulness of the terminology, examples, and content used. Novices of above-average ability or of broader experience can provide useful feedback about alternative content, learning procedures, and examples, as well.

Stakeholders

The third type of evaluator, commonly called a *stakeholder,* is all too often ignored. Stakeholders are people affected in one way or another by a particular product under development. We ought to solicit evaluative advice from representatives of such groups during the development process. They can help us avoid any unintentional content omissions or errors or practices that may be outdated or offensive to them, and they may suggest content, activities, and materials of particular value or use to them. Thus, for example, we should enlist representatives of various ethnic or cultural groups as expert evaluators of an elementary school language arts curriculum or textbook. We should also solicit feedback from representatives of various geographic regions or localities within the community, among others.

In our search for stakeholders to include, we should not forget *gatekeepers.* Gatekeepers are people who, because of their position or influence, can affect decisions about the use of particular kinds of educational products. For example, if we are developing a sex education program, we should be sure to solicit feedback from representatives of racial, ethnic, gender, and religious groups; parent groups; and professional or social agencies. Advice from these groups will not only enable us to produce a better quality program, but it may well also help us avoid or minimize controversy and build support in the community for the final product (Edgemon and Thomas 1979). Because of their special expertise or point of view or experience, certain gatekeepers can make valuable contributions and in the process, perhaps, become strong supporters of the final product.

Numbers of Evaluators

Obviously, not all evaluators can provide information relevant to all of the kinds of information that we need. Learners or users, for example, are hardly sufficient judges of the accuracy of content, especially if it is new to them. Subject-matter experts are often not the best judges of the clarity of task directions or of teaching strategies. Thus, any educational product development effort should involve different kinds of evaluators because each kind can provide different perspectives and information that we need to produce a quality product. No single evaluator can provide useful insights into all aspects of a product.

In developing an educational product or program, therefore, we should enlist the services of different people in our formative evaluation.

Evaluating a Textbook/An Example of Appropriate Evaluators

If we are developing a textbook, for example, our formative evaluators at the design stage might include several experts in content and cognition, several experienced potential users, and several significant stakeholders.

At the prototype or pilot stage of the textbook, evaluators might include two to three experts (with expertise in the subject matter of the planned text, in learning theory and cognition, and in instruction), three students at the intended grade level (one each of low, average, and high ability), an experienced teacher of the subject, and a beginning teacher of the subject—all for the pilot testing of the product.

For field trials of the textbook, we should employ classes (and teachers) totaling 90 or more students typical of the "target" student population. The formative evaluators should also include gatekeepers whose values and perspectives we need to consider. At the very least, we should include representatives of relevant secondary users or interest groups in the field trials.

Evaluating a How-to Manual/Another Example

To provide another example, suppose we are developing a manual for secondary school administrators on how to establish and maintain site-based management of a high school. For the formative evaluation, we might enlist the services of 6 to 20 people, including at least 3 experts, such as someone experienced in bringing about change in educational institutions, a specialist in site-based management, and a secondary school administrator successful in site-based management. This project could also use the services of 2 or 3 secondary school principals with varied experiences to pilot test the manual and perhaps more if different types of secondary schools (rural, urban, suburban) were subjects of the manual. A larger number of representative school administrators should also try out the completed, revised manual in field trials.

Use of a Review Panel

Where pilot or field trials are impossible because of the nature of the product being developed, evaluators may be organized into groups, often called panels, to provide the desired feedback. Several organizations developing national standards of learning in different K–12 curriculum areas have recently taken such an approach. For example, the Standards Development Task Force of the National Council for the Social Studies submitted successive drafts of its proposed standards to five different panels of evaluators:

- A panel of professional association leaders
- A national panel of social studies teachers
- A national panel of educational associations and civic, community, business, and government groups
- A panel of student groups
- A panel of 800 schools representative of the nation's private and public schools

As the standards moved through development and revision toward a final document, the task force incorporated the feedback that each panel generated (Task Force, National Council for the Social Studies 1993).

From these examples, we can see that a formative evaluation requires no magic number of participants. The number of evaluators often depends on the knowledge and experience of the individual experts participating. The nature of a development effort also affects the number of evaluators needed—for example, the development of computer software obviously requires different kinds of evaluators from those required to assess national education standards. The kinds and amount of resources that can be devoted to an evaluation effort also affect the exact number of evaluators involved.

As the textbook, manual, and review panel examples show, any development effort needs *more than one expert*—at least one in the content of the product and one in the method of delivering the content—and at least *one or two gatekeepers or stakeholders,* as well as *enough users representative of the target audience* to give a valid sense of whether the product will actually work as intended.

Working with Expert Evaluators

We must look beyond numbers in selecting expert evaluators for our programs or products. The following are guidelines to follow in selecting experts and soliciting their feedback:

1. Select evaluators clearly qualified as experts. What makes an expert an expert? An expert is one who has demonstrated over time a high degree of skill, knowledge, or competence in a subject or field as attested by peer recognition and by a record of producing high-quality products, essays, and other works in the field. When we put together a team for a formative evaluation, we must make sure that the experts are not simply friends or superiors. The credentials of the evaluators must clearly establish them as recognized experts in their fields.

2. Whenever possible, we should look for people who combine multiple areas of expertise. It is not necessary to match each area of needed expertise with a different evaluator. An expert in risk management, for example, may also be a successful school administrator and thus might supply valuable feedback in our effort to develop a manual on risk management for secondary school administrators.

3. We must also make sure that evaluators understand the nature and scope of our development effort and have a good sense of the time involved. In securing and managing expert evaluation, we may encounter problems with evaluations that are not thorough enough or that do not meet our timelines. Though we cannot eliminate such problems altogether, we can take some actions to minimize them.

The Expert's Need to Know

Sometimes, expert evaluators—especially those who volunteer because of personal friendship or are volunteered by their superiors or grudgingly acquiesce out of an externally stimulated sense of responsibility—provide only superficial or perfunctory feedback. Occasionally, their responses arrive too late to be helpful in revising the product for the next trial or assessment cycle. These situations can be caused by, among other things:

- An expert evaluator's failure to know what the developer really needs or wishes to know as a result of the expert evaluations
- A lack (or perceived lack) of time to devote to doing the evaluation
- A lack of commitment to the value of the product being developed
- A failure to understand the importance of how the evaluative feedback will be used and how it could shape the final product

Fortunately, we can eliminate or minimize delays caused by any of those conditions.

We simply cannot assume that experts enlisted for formative evaluation know the kinds of judgments or information or the amount of detail that we need most at any given point in the development process. Nor can we assume that expert evaluators are going to drop everything when they receive the material to be evaluated and turn immediately to the evaluation task. However, to help ensure timely and thorough expert evaluations, we should take these measures:

- Inform potential evaluators of their exact role in the development process and the significance of the contributions they can make to the quality of the final product.
- Inform potential evaluators in advance—when their assistance is first sought—of the time their evaluation tasks will probably require, the dates they will receive the material, and the dates their evaluations are due; also keep them abreast of changes in those dates.

• Show potential experts samples of the kinds of reports and responses—and of the details expected in each—that they will be asked to submit.

• Provide detailed, specific prompts, questions, and tasks for the evaluators to complete or do, limiting the amount of free-response writing required by using focused checklists, short-answer items, and structured prompts.

• Allow an appropriate amount of time (2 to 3 weeks) for experts to complete their evaluations.

• Alert evaluators 1 or 2 weeks ahead of the intended arrival date of the material they are to evaluate; at the same time, give them the deadline for responding.

• Check with evaluators several days after they have received the material to be sure it has arrived and to see if they have any questions or need any clarification of their tasks; volunteer to be readily available for questions as they arise.

• If the development effort is sponsored by an organization some of whose employees are the evaluators, make proceeding to the next stage of the development process contingent on timely return of acceptable evaluations and feedback.

• Provide incentives for timely and appropriately detailed evaluations and feedback, such as the following:

–honoraria, fees, or stipends;
–reduced work loads;
–time off from regular work;
–meals or refreshments during debriefing sessions, interviews, or other meetings;
–free (classroom) sets of the final version of the product or training in how to use it;
–listing of evaluator names in the credits and acknowledgments attached to the final product and in any publications related to it.

• Conduct all expert evaluations at the design stage simultaneously; at the prototype, pilot, or field trial stages, conduct them simultaneously with user evaluations.

The Importance of Being Timely

Whatever techniques we use to ensure the quality of expert evaluations, we can benefit from following these important guidelines:

• Be realistic and upfront about the amount of time allowed for preparing each formative evaluation.

• Before beginning the development process, secure a commitment from each evaluator to do a thorough and timely job.

• Allow enough time for experts to do the required evaluations, given all their regular commitments.

• Have backup experts lined up just in case first-choice evaluators change their minds or do not do the kind of evaluation needed.

We should not underestimate the value of top-quality expert evaluations during all stages of the development process. Nor should we underestimate the difficulties in arranging and monitoring those evaluations. Being considerate of evaluators will go a long way toward ensuring quality and timeliness of their contributions to a project.

Developer-Based Evaluation

Outside expert evaluators are not the only source of expert formative feedback in the development process. As developers, we can reliably evaluate our own work, especially when we analyze and judge how well our products meet already existing, commonly used standards. Those standards may be articulated by professional organizations, by specialists, or by special interest groups related to the kind of product under development.

If we are developing a textbook, for example, we can use evaluation checklists developed by expert text evaluators—such as Meredith Gall's widely used textbook evaluation matrix (Borg and Gall 1989). Furthermore, many K–12 subject-matter organizations, such as the National Council for the Social Studies, have developed content standards and guidelines that can also serve as checklists for evaluating curriculums, texts, or other instructional materials.

In addition, we can use the results of accumulated research as criteria for making evaluative judgments, especially at the design stage of product development. For example, James Raths (1971) conducted an extensive analysis of research studies on teaching and synthesized a set of guidelines for selecting and using different kinds of teaching and learning strategies. According to Raths, research indicates that one learning activity is more worthwhile than another if the proposed activity:

• Allows students to make informed choices in carrying out the activity and to reflect on the consequences of their choices

• Gives students active, rather than passive, roles in learning

• Enables students to inquire into ideas, applications of intellectual process, or current problems, either intellectual or social

• Involves students with *realia* (actual material rather than abstract representations of such material)

• Can be completed successfully by children at several different levels of ability

• Has students examine in a new setting an idea, an application of an intellectual process, or a current problem studied previously

• Requires students to examine topics or issues not normally examined by citizens or focused on by the media, such as the profit motive, homelessness, and foreign influences on American media

• Involves risk of success or failure for the students and teachers involved

• Requires students to rehearse, revise, and polish their initial efforts

• Involves students in sharing with others the planning, the execution of a plan, or the results of an activity

• Relates to the expressed purposes of the students

As developers, we can use solidly based standards, such as this synthesis by Raths, as criteria for judging which strategies to include in most instructional programs without recourse to the services of outside experts.

We may find other standards helpful, as well. For example, learning specialist Hilda Taba (1962) articulated the essential elements of concept teaching and learning.

During a distinguished career as a developer of a wide range of innovative instructional programs and materials, Edwin Fenton (n.d.) proposed and used an extensive list of standards for judging the quality of instructional materials before submitting them to classroom tryout. Figure 3.1 (see the next page) contains these standards in the form of questions, adapted and generalized to apply to virtually any kind of educational product. We can use these questions to determine the potential workability and quality of a newly developed curriculum, course, textbook, learning program, or other type of educational product *before* it is even submitted to any kind of expert, prototype, pilot, or field tryout.

We can also use these and other relevant published standards as checklists in evaluating our own work at appropriate places in the development process. Using such checklists before actual tryout can prevent costly and embarrassing errors later in the development cycle. If independent evaluators use such standards in an honest, candid fashion, we will likely see marked improvements in the quality of our products early in the development process.

Figure 3.1

Design and Development Checklist

1. How does a lesson, chapter, unit, or component fit in the scheme of an entire sequence of lessons, text, program, or course?

2. To what extent does each component have a clear, unifying theme?

3. How well do the learning activities in a chapter, unit, or segment relate clearly to each other?

4. Does the product contain sufficient variety?

5. How long will it take to work with the material during class?

6. What specific prior knowledge or skills does the material or product presuppose?

7. Is the reading level appropriate to the intended audience?

8. Are the number and difficulty of the questions appropriate?

9. Are the objectives of each piece of media clear?

10. Are the learning objectives stated as clearly as possible?

11. Are the materials appropriate for attaining the specified objectives?

12. Can those objectives be reached with the suggested teaching techniques and materials?

Note: Adapted from Edwin Fenton (n.d.).

From Barry K. Beyer, *How to Conduct a Formative Evaluation* (Alexandria, Va.: Association for Supervision and Curriculum Development, 1995).

4
Data-Gathering Instruments and Procedures

IN CONDUCTING FORMATIVE EVALUATIONS, WE CAN USE AN
impressive array of procedures and instruments, including
the following:

- Annotated analyses of print materials
- Questionnaires
- Quantitative performance or achievement assessments
- Examination of user-produced products
- Learning, teaching, and using logs
- Error logs
- Observations
- Interviews
- Focus groups
- Video and audio recordings
- Anecdotal records
- Open-ended critiques or reports

No matter which formative evaluation procedures or
instruments we do select, we should sure they are
user-friendly and explicit. If there is one thing that
evaluators don't do well, it is voluntarily write a lot or
provide on their own initiative the kinds of information we
often really need. Nor do all volunteer evaluators,
especially, seem inclined to give products as close an
examination as we might like.

Here, then, are 12 procedures or types of instruments
especially useful in the formative evaluation of educational
products, with suggestions on how to design or use them.

Annotation of Materials

One of the most useful formative evaluation procedures in the development of print materials is for experts and users to mark up and annotate print materials as they examine or use them. Annotations can pinpoint gaps or errors in content, lack of clarity, inappropriate use of words or phrases, lack of examples or suggestions for additional or other examples, or desirable changes in content and structure, right at the points where changes would be useful. Student users and other evaluators can also follow this procedure. No other form of formative evaluation offers the potential for such specific and useful feedback as does the annotation of print material.

In our instructions for these annotations, we should direct the evaluators' attention to specific topics by giving precise tasks for them to complete. For example, if we ask experts to evaluate a draft of a textbook, we can provide the following directions:

As you read this draft, please:

• Bracket [ ] any statements that are unclear, and mark or rewrite them to make them clearer.

• Cross out any statements you consider inaccurate, and note in the margin the correct version—or a source to go to make it accurate.

• Put a caret ^ to indicate something that should be there but isn't, and note in the margin what should be inserted.

• Draw an arrow → to indicate the place where something should be moved to facilitate use or learning or to clarify the material.

• Circle any statement or section that you believe to be beyond the understanding of the user, and note in the margin what might be done to improve it.

Annotations like these pinpoint important things we need to know before the product is put into final form. Use of symbols minimizes the need for considerable writing, yet allows the evaluators to provide the information. Of course, evaluators can also be invited—indeed, strongly encouraged—to write as many marginal notes, suggestions, or questions as they believe may be helpful in improving the quality of the product.

Providing evaluators a limited number of symbols to use produces more helpful feedback than we might otherwise get. By repeating the directions periodically throughout the material, we can also help the expert evaluators keep focused on what they are supposed to be doing.

Student users of print material—and even software programs—can also annotate and mark up material as they use it, if directed explicitly to do so. For example, we might give these directions to student users of a pilot version of any print learning material:

As you use this material, please:

• Circle any words or phrases that you do not understand.

• In the margin, write *EX* when you believe one or more examples would help you better understand what has just been stated. Writing a brief suggestion of a good example in the margin will also be most helpful.

• Put a question mark ? in the margin next to anything that is not clear to you. Making a note in the margin telling specifically what needs to be cleared up will help.

Keep in mind one caution in giving evaluators directions for annotating drafts of written products: Having evaluators be responsible for too many items to look for or too many symbols to use in making annotations may prevent them from focusing on the text of the product itself. One way to deal with that is to recommend multiple examinations (readings) of the product, with the evaluator looking at only a limited number of variables each time. Another way is to intersperse in the print material being evaluated a list of the variables to look for or symbols to use. Or we can provide a card with that information on it for the evaluator to keep visible throughout the evaluation process.

Of course, specifying certain things for evaluators to look for in examining a product should not preclude them from commenting on any other features they might wish to mention. Experienced evaluators may be sensitive to some crucial factors or development issues that the formative evaluation designers may have overlooked. Their voluntary observations sometimes alert us to important issues that for any number of reasons we may have ignored or have been insensitive to up to that point. Encouraging open-ended annotative comments and suggestions is a useful adjunct to highly structured or explicit directions.

Questionnaires

Questionnaires prove extremely useful in formative evaluation. A list of questions can ask for specific information as well as judgments; and the evaluators can be directed to specific sections, components, features, or segments of a product. In this way, we can make changes based on the responses. A questionnaire like the one in Figure 4.1 (see pp. 37–41) is thus preferable to a questionnaire that asks only for unsubstantiated ways to revise items identified as problems or that are general in nature. General questions fail to identify specifically where changes should be made; opinions or judgments unsupported by recommended revisions fail to help developers pinpoint where and exactly what revisions may be useful.

The questionnaire in Figure 4.1 provides detailed instructions for the user, ties each question to specified evaluation objectives, and allows opportunity and space for free responses and suggestions. Starting with item 10, the questions are keyed to specific pages in the materials being evaluated; some questions, like item 19, actually direct the user where to make appropriate annotations on the material. By relating questions to specific points in or components of the material, we can virtually guarantee receiving feedback that will be immediately helpful in correcting errors, closing gaps, and eliminating irrelevancies in the product being developed.

FIGURE 4.1

A Formative Evaluation Questionnaire

Name: _____ Position: _____

1. Skim the attached formative evaluation questionnaire before you read the instructional materials. Note the kind of information you are asked to supply.

2. Read carefully through the *Instructor's Guide* and the *Student Handbook*.

3. As you read these materials, annotate the pages with any comments, questions, or corrections.

4. Then, answer the questionnaire and provide written comments if possible. However, there may be some responses that you prefer to discuss with me personally rather than writing them. When you have finished the questionnaire, I will schedule a conference with you to discuss your responses. Thank you for assisting me. I appreciate your willingess to give me both your expertise and your valuable personal time.

Instructions: Place written responses in the space below each question. Use the back of the page if necessary.

Objective 1: **To determine the appropriateness of the course objectives.**

1. Are the course objectives appropriate for a business and professional communication course? If not, please indicate what needs to be deleted or changed.

By the end of this course, the students will be able to:

Objective 1: Demonstrate understanding of organizational communication theories and practices through class discussion, written examination, and speaking assignments.

YES [ ] NO [ ]

(Continued on the next page)

EXPERT FORMATIVE EVALUATION

Objectives:
1. To determine the appropriateness of the course objectives.
2. To determine the appropriateness of the course design.
3. To determine the accuracy and currency of the content.
4. To determine the appropriateness of communication skill teaching methods.
5. To determine the clarity and appropriateness of the instructional materials.

Materials:

The materials for the formative evaluation include an *Instructor's Guide* and a *Student Handbook*. The *Instructor's Guide* contains the philosophical overview of the course, syllabus, schedule, lesson plans, lecture notes, quizzes, and storyboard for a videotape of model business communication presentations. The *Student Handbook* is intended to supplement any business communication textbook used for the course. The *Handbook* contains the practice communication simulations, supplementary information to understand the simulations, presentation assignments, and peer and self-evaluations. The lesson plans in the *Instructor's Guide* indicate how these materials are used during the class sessions and for homework assignments.

Suggested Evaluation Procedures:

The questionnaire I have prepared is very detailed so that I can obtain specific information that will enable me to revise the course and materials for the purpose of increasing student learning. To facilitate the evaluation process for you, I recommend the following procedure:

From Barry K. Beyer, *How to Conduct a Formative Evaluation* (Alexandria, Va.: Association for Supervision and Curriculum Development, 1995). Copyright © 1995 by Barry K. Beyer. Charts and figures may be reproduced for educational purposes only.

FIGURE 4.1—*Continued*

38

Objective 2: Plan, monitor, and assess self-improvement for oral presentations.

YES [ ]   NO [ ]

Objective 3: Demonstrate effective active listening strategies during interviews, group meetings, and public presentations.

YES [ ]   NO [ ]

Objective 4: Demonstrate effective one-to-one oral communication strategies for conducting a performance appraisal interview.

YES [ ]   NO [ ]

Objective 5: Demonstrate effective oral skills as a leader and member of a problem-solving group meeting.

YES [ ]   NO [ ]

Objective 6: Demonstrate effective public speaking techniques for persuasive business presentations.

YES [ ]   NO [ ]

Objective 7: Demonstrate knowledge of effective oral communication principles through written and oral peer evaluations of interview, small-group, and public speech presentations.

YES [ ]   NO [ ]

2. Are the performance objectives for the three communication units consistent with the course objectives listed in question 1? If not, please note which are inconsistent.

Unit 3: Performance Appraisal Interview Objectives
(*Handbook*, p. 3–1)

YES [ ]   NO [ ]

Unit 4: Small-Group Communication
(*Handbook*, p. 4–1)

YES [ ]   NO [ ]

Unit 5: Persuasive Speech
(*Handbook*, p. 5–1)

YES [ ]   NO [ ]

Objective 2: To determine the appropriateness of the course design for the learner.

3. Have entry-level skills and abilities of learners been considered sufficiently in the design of this course? If not, what skills and abilities have not been considered?

YES [ ]   NO [ ]

4. Is the pace of instruction appropriate for the learners? (See Course Schedule in the *Instructor's Guide*.) If not, please suggest ways to improve the pace.

YES [ ]   NO [ ]

5. Does the course provide an appropriate amount of challenge to learners (undergraduate juniors and seniors)? If not, what can be done to provide more challenge?

YES [ ]   NO [ ]

Objective 3: To determine the accuracy and currency of the content.

6. Are there any obvious gaps in the information provided in the following *Handbook* units? Please note what information is missing.

Unit 3:   YES [ ]   NO [ ]
Unit 4:   YES [ ]   NO [ ]
Unit 5:   YES [ ]   NO [ ]

FIGURE 4.1—*Continued*

7. Are there any inaccuracies in any of the *Student Handbook* units? If so, please note needed corrections.

Unit 3:   YES [ ]   NO [ ]
Unit 4:   YES [ ]   NO [ ]
Unit 5:   YES [ ]   NO [ ]

8. Is there any irrelevant information in the *Handbook* units? If so, please note the information that is unnecessary.

Unit 3:   YES [ ]   NO [ ]
Unit 4:   YES [ ]   NO [ ]
Unit 5:   YES [ ]   NO [ ]

9. Are the speaking assignments (appraisal interviewing, problem-solving discussion, and persuasive speech) the most relevant business presentations to learn? If not, what kinds of speaking assignments might be more relevant?

    YES [ ]   NO [ ]

Objective 4: To determine the appropriateness of the communication skills instructional methods.

10. Is the instructional sequence (order) for presenting information within each unit appropriate? If not, please indicate what changes should be made.

Unit 3: Performance Appraisal interview (Contents, p 3-ii)   YES [ ]   NO [ ]

Unit 4: Small-Group Discussion (Contents, p. 4-i)   YES [ ]   NO [ ]

Unit 5: Persuasive Speech Presentation (Contents, p. 5-i)   YES [ ]   NO [ ]

11. Is the overall instructional sequence (first, performance appraisal interview; second, problem-solving discussion; and third, persuasive speech) appropriate?   YES [ ]   NO [ ]

12. Are the following instructional strategies for teaching oral communication skills appropriate? If not, please suggest changes to make them more appropriate.

Goal setting, p 3-2 to 3-6   YES [ ]   NO [ ]
Goal monitoring, p. 3-7 to 3-9   YES [ ]   NO [ ]
Goal assessing, p. 3-10   YES [ ]   NO [ ]
Directive lesson structure (See lesson plans, *Instructor's Guide*)   YES [ ]   NO [ ]
Videotaped presentation models (See storyboard, *Instructor's Guide*)   YES [ ]   NO [ ]
Practice simulations, pp. 13–15, 4–11, 5–12, 22   YES [ ]   NO [ ]
Learning points, pp. 3–14, 4–10, 5–10, 11   YES [ ]   NO [ ]
Videotaping student presentations   YES [ ]   NO [ ]
Peer evaluation, pp. 3–28, 4–30 & 31, 5–37   YES [ ]   NO [ ]
Self-evaluation, pp. 3–28, 4–29, 5–38   YES [ ]   NO [ ]

(Continued on the next page)

From Barry K. Beyer, *How to Conduct a Formative Evaluation* (Alexandria, Va.: Association for Supervision and Curriculum Development, 1995). Copyright © 1995 by Barry K. Beyer. Charts and figures may be reproduced for educational purposes only.

FIGURE 4.1—Continued

13. Do the in-class practice exercises prepare the students sufficiently for the corresponding presentation assignment? If not, what changes do you recommend?

Interview practice simulation, p. 3–15   YES [ ]   NO [ ]
Interview assignment, p. 3–20

Problem-solving simulation, p. 4–11   YES [ ]   NO [ ]
Problem-solving assignment, p. 4–22

Practice simulation 1, p. 5–12   YES [ ]   NO [ ]
Persuasive assignment, p. 5–25

Practice simulation 2, p. 5–22   YES [ ]   NO [ ]
Persuasive assignment, p. 5–25

14. Do the above practice simulations and the presentation assignments develop sufficiently the five oral communication skills (verbal language, nonverbal behavior, message organization, delivery, and listening), which are the learning outcomes of this course? If not, what changes do you recommend?

Performance appraisal interview   YES [ ]   NO [ ]
Problem-solving group discussion   YES [ ]   NO [ ]
Persuasive speech   YES [ ]   NO [ ]

Objective 5: To determine the appropriateness of the instructional materials.

15. Is the vocabulary in the *Student Handbook* clear? Underline unclear vocabulary on the instruction materials.

    YES [ ]   NO [ ]

16. Do the learning point charts present the key components for each of the five oral communication skills as they are applied to the specific type of presentation? If not, please note any changes needed.

Performance appraisal learning points,   YES [ ]   NO [ ]
p. 3–14

Problem-solving discussion learning points,   YES [ ]   NO [ ]
p. 4–10

Persuasive speech learning points,   YES [ ]   NO [ ]
p. 5–10

Active listening learning points, p.   YES [ ]   NO [ ]
5–11

17. Do the peer evaluation forms evaluate the five communication skills appropriately? If not, what changes do you recommend?

Interview peer evaluation, p. 3–30   YES [ ]   NO [ ]

Group-discussion evaluations,   YES [ ]   NO [ ]
pp. 4–30, 31.

Persuasive speech evaluation,   YES [ ]   NO [ ]
p. 5–37

18. Are the quiz instructions, vocabulary, questions, and response expectations clear? If not, underline any unclear items. (See *Instructor's Guide.*)

Unit 3 quiz   YES [ ]   NO [ ]
Unit 4 quiz   YES [ ]   NO [ ]
Unit 5 quiz   YES [ ]   NO [ ]

From Barry K. Beyer, *How to Conduct a Formative Evaluation* (Alexandria, Va.: Association for Supervision and Curriculum Development, 1995). Copyright © 1995 by Barry K. Beyer. Charts and figures may be reproduced for educational purposes only.

FIGURE 4.1—*Continued*

19. Do the quizzes assess the stated unit performance objectives? If not, circle the number of the question that does not seem appropriate.

    Unit 3 quiz   YES [ ]   NO [ ]

    Unit 4 quiz   YES [ ]   NO [ ]

    Unit 5 quiz   YES [ ]   NO [ ]

20. Is the content of the proposed videotape appropriate and well structured? (See storyboard in the *Instructor's Guide*.) If not, what changes do you recommend?

                                    YES [ ]   NO [ ]

21. Can another instructor easily use these materials as printed? If not, what changes do you recommend to make them more usable?

    Practice simulations   YES [ ]   NO [ ]

    Communication activities   YES [ ]   NO [ ]

    Presentation assignments   YES [ ]   NO [ ]

    Peer evaluation forms   YES [ ]   NO [ ]

CONCLUDING ASSESSMENT

22. Please add any other comments or suggestions that would improve the course or instructional materials.

Note: Adapted by permission from Jayne S. Lytle, *Professional Presentations: Design and Evaluation of an Oral Communication Skills Course.* Unpublished doctoral dissertation, George Mason University (1991), pp. 354–361.

From Barry K. Beyer, *How to Conduct a Formative Evaluation* (Alexandria, Va.: Association for Supervision and Curriculum Development, 1995). Copyright © 1995 by Barry K. Beyer. Charts and figures may be reproduced for educational purposes only.

In planning to use questionnaires to secure formative feedback, we should remember that many evaluators, whether experts or novice users:

- Don't know what we as developers need or want to know,
- Don't like to write or read very much, and
- Don't respond with details or specifics to most open-ended questions.

Therefore, evaluators should be provided with specially designed instruments keyed to specific components, segments, or features of the product. These should include specific directions and prompts, clearly defined criteria, and reminders of what the evaluators are to look for. Instruments, questions, or tasks should focus on specific variables or components. Short-answer questions are preferable to completely open-ended ones.

Unless followed immediately by requests for suggested corrections, additional information, or desirable modifications, *opinion questions* usually produce little information useful for formative purposes. Such questions often fail to provide information specific enough to generate effective alterations in the original.

Further, as good as many experts or specialists may be in their fields, few are experienced enough at formative evaluation to attend simultaneously to more than one or two variables or features to be evaluated. Nor are they always willing—unless reimbursed in some way for their services—to examine something more than once, attending to a different variable each time. Thus, when we give newly developed materials to evaluators for feedback, we should provide regular and frequent reminders of what they are to look for (inserts or cards, as mentioned previously).

Not all formative evaluation questionnaires need be in the conventional question-blank-space–question-blank-space format. To save space and to make it easier for respondents, some questionnaires might be constructed as checklists or presented in chart form, as in Figure 4.2. This figure presents a format for securing formative feedback on the quality of learning objectives in a hypothetical course under development. It minimizes the need for respondents to write a great deal, directs them to make judgments about the objectives in terms of specific criteria, and asks for suggestions for improving anything felt to be less than adequate.

FIGURE 4.2

Example Expert Formative Evaluation of Learning Objectives

Mark X if item is not:	Clearly stated	Appropriate for learning this content	Appropriate for the intended students	Suggested Revisions
Objective 1				
Objective 2				
Objective 3				
Objective 4				

From Barry K. Beyer, *How to Conduct a Formative Evaluation* (Alexandria, Va.: Association for Supervision and Curriculum Development, 1995). Copyright © 1995 by Barry K. Beyer. Charts and figures may be reproduced for educational purposes only.

Quantitative Performance and Achievement Assessments

Assessing user behaviors or the effects of the product or program on users is essential—for instance, measuring math achievement levels after students field test a new computer-assisted math program we may have developed. Achievement assessment provides the most convincing evidence of the quality of that product. Such assessments may be in the form of paper-and-pencil objective measures of recall or application of information or other types of objectively assessed performances. The latter may include measures of analytical or problem-solving or decision-making abilities, of conceptualizing or writing abilities, or of any other kind of skilled performances, mastery of which has been an objective of the product being evaluated. We can use quantified results of these assessments to determine how well the product—as a whole and its individual components—enables users to achieve the learning objectives of the product.

Because the intent of quantifiable measurement in formative evaluation is to determine how well a product achieves its objectives, effective use of these measures is limited to the final stage of the development process—the field trials. In field tests, large numbers of users use the product in the context for which it was designed. By this stage, we should have removed all the previously identified bugs and provided any special training in the product's use or administration.

In using objective measures, we should follow four important guidelines:

• *If the measures are being created for evaluating a new product, they must themselves go through the same kind of development process, including formative evaluation, as the product is going through.* That is, newly created performance assessment instruments or procedures must be submitted for formative evaluation to experts in content and assessment, then revised based on that feedback, administered as prototypes to a sample of actual potential users, and then revised and retried again by a small sample of potential users. This procedure may, in fact, have to be repeated several times until workable, valid, and reliable instruments or procedures are developed. Only after the assessment procedures or instruments have gone through this process can they be trusted to provide reliable, valid formative evaluation data.

• *To be most effective, the components of any quantifiable measure must be keyed to specific elements of the product being assessed, so that unacceptable results on any part of the measure can pinpoint exactly where in the product corrective changes need to be made.* Thus, for example, an instrument assessing decision-making performance must be organized so that it clearly pinpoints the various elements of decision making presented in the material. Generalized or vague quantifiable measures do not provide feedback that is especially useful for revising educational materials under development.

• *Assessment instruments and performance requirements must be congruent with the objectives of the product being evaluated, its content, and other features.* Without congruence between what is developed by a program and what is assessed, the results of the assessment will be worthless (Borg 1987).

• *In most cases, administer quantifiable measures of achievement or performance both before and after evaluators have used the product.* This way, any significant differences can be attributed to using the product itself. To be more certain of that, the same measures can also be administered to control groups who do not use the product.

For formative evaluation purposes, however, we don't necessarily need to establish comparison groups using similar or substitute products. Such comparative assessment addresses a question other than the key formative evaluation question of: *How well does using this product as directed achieve the objectives set?* Unless a goal of a particular new product is that its use achieves certain objectives *better* than do other similar products, a comparative evaluation design is unnecessary. Even if such an evaluation is deemed useful, formative evaluation calls first for assessing how well a new product works. Only after answering that question does it prove worthwhile or wise to assess the comparative quality of a newly developed product.

Quantifiable performance or achievement measures do prove useful in formative evaluation. But they are best used in the later stages of the development process. And while carefully constructed and analyzed quantitative evaluation instruments can provide useful formative feedback, they do not by any means provide all the kinds of information we need—such as workability of various materials, clarity of directions, content accuracy, and sequence (Stenhouse 1988).

Examination of User-Produced Products

Analyzing what students produce as a result of using a product or participating in a program under development can also help improve the quality of a product, whether it be a textbook program, a piece of software, or even a course or collection of courses. For example, analysis of reports or papers prepared by representative learners can give insights into the following:

- The clarity of directions
- How valid assumptions are about the skills and knowledge learners bring to the program or develop as a result of using the product
- Gaps in information or skill training included in the program up to that point

Learner-produced products that meet the intended objectives and standards of quality of the product provide excellent testimony of the product's quality up to that point.

Learning, Teaching, and Using Logs

Logs are open-ended, usually free-response records kept by users as they use a product. Logs can be kept by learners, instructors, or anyone who uses a product at any level. Although learning logs may consist of highly specific prompts, the most useful logs leave respondents free to also indicate their own spontaneous and personal reflections, reactions, suggestions, or anecdotal observations or comments. Such information in the aggregate provides clues to areas where changes are needed and frequently also provides creative suggestions for making those changes.

A typical learning log to accompany an educational program might include the following prompts and accompanying instructions:

Complete each of the following in a sentence or two as you reflect on the activity, lesson, or task that you just completed:

1. I learned . . .
2. I wonder . . .
3. I am surprised . . .
4. I wish . . .
5. I think . . .
6. I suggest . . . because . . .

Although each of these prompts seeks a particular kind of response, none forces any specific comment. Responses to "I learned" generally turn out to be about what was learned as a result of completing the task—but often rather than specifying a content learning, respondents will comment on the learning conditions ("I learned . . . that I don't learn so well when the room is hot"), quality of the material, or some incident that occurred during the activity.

Responses to "I wonder" prompts usually appear in the form of questions that may need to be answered in a revision of the product.

"I am surprised," "I wish," "I suggest," and similar responses often appear as ideas or results or consequences that we may not have anticipated. These "surprises" are often useful in improving the product's quality (e.g., "I'm surprised . . . that there isn't a map—it would help me understand where all the places mentioned are"). We may also devise additional prompts to match a particular type of product or to elicit reactions on a particular topic.

Error Logs

Sometimes called "bug logs," error logs are written commentaries that point out errors or problems identified in the process of attempting to use a new product for the first time. Log entries may take the form of anecdotal records with a focus on bugs or errors identified by users or experts as they work with the product. Or error logs may be responses to questions posed in ongoing interviews of users during trial uses of the product. Error logs also may consist of the records kept by trained evaluators observing the trial use of a product. Such a log can even be generated by the program management system of a computer-based instructional program—for example, by recording the number of tries required of users or the errors made by users in carrying out each task in a program.

One way to structure an error log for users is to accompany each activity or component of a product with a series of questions like these:

1. What problem, error, bug occurred?
2. Exactly what happened?
3. Where—or when—in the material did it occur?
4. Why do you believe it happened?
5. What did you do to resolve it?
6. What else do you think could be done to resolve it?

A log using such prompts to evaluate a piece of educational software, for example, can alert us to errors in sequencing of frames or to errors in responding to incorrect student inputs. Regardless of the form they take, the purpose of error logs is to identify user problems with the product and to suggest ways to remedy those problems. Such logs are invaluable sources of feedback for improving the quality of any product during its development.

Observation

Observations of a product being used on a trial basis should be shaped by the stage of development and the specific things we are trying to find out at that point. Thus, an observation of a colleague attempting to use a prototype of a new computer program should focus on the mechanics of operating the program rather than on what is learned or how enjoyable it is to the user. Observations of representative users of a pilot version of the software might well focus on different concerns. Although open-ended observation may prove useful if the observers are the developers and know what to look for, checklists are valuable for focusing observation on the kinds of information that developers need most.

One particularly useful form of observation occurs in one-on-one tryout of a draft or prototype of a newly developed product. For example, we (or someone else who is familiar with the product) can sit with a novice user of a new computer program while the learner uses the product as directed, step by step. In doing this, we need to watch carefully as the user follows directions for the computer program, to note and record user errors or problems when they arise, and to ask questions—when the user appears confused or errs or is stuck and inquiring—and record responses—*why* the user made dysfunctional or erroneous or unanticipated moves.

During these one-on-one sessions, we may also record the time it takes to complete a task or its subtasks, the questions the user asks while trying to make sense of directions or content, and the reasons the user gives for any false, confused, or unusual moves. This is an intense but a productive type of formative evaluation, especially when conducted with several representative users in turn.

In conducting one-on-one observations, we should include several trials, each with a different type of user or learner (Borg 1987). Dick and Carey (1985) recommend, for example, that, especially in the trials of prototypes where such kinds of product evaluation are essential, subjects conduct separate run-throughs, in turn, with at least one above-average user and one below-average user. Close monitoring of how each kind of user engages with the new product can reveal all kinds of problems.

Above-average users often prove adept at suggesting useful modifications or options. Below-average users, in their sometimes painful struggle to use the product, can reveal problems with directions, language or task difficulty, ambiguity of content, and so on. With a little probing, we can often find solutions to such problems on the spot.

Exactly what an observer should do in any particular one-on-one observation may vary, but some general guidelines apply:

• Explain to users that the sample material is in draft form and will be revised based on their reactions and suggestions. Encourage them to ask questions and report any difficulties in using the product.

• Note any errors pointed out or confusion that users encountered, and record what they did in response.

• Note any places where users requested help and why they made the request. Note also the nature of the help given and how well it worked.

• When users are confronted with a problem, have them talk through solving it or suggest ways the product can be improved to resolve the problem.

• Encourage users to comment aloud about the product as they are using it, especially about directions, words used, task requirements and operations, examples that might be helpful, what they are doing, and why.

• Note any evidence of the user's attitudes toward the product—for example, "shows interest or disinterest," their degree of engagement, or mechanistic behavior.

In a debriefing session after a one-on-one trial, we may find it useful to have the user summarize reactions to the product, tell what has been learned from it, note its strengths and weaknesses, and suggest ways the product could be made more informative, useful, efficient or meaningful.

Three important factors about observation are worthy of special note:

• Multiple observers of the same event provide much richer information than does a single observer. When several observers debrief together, they invariably compare and discuss what they observed from different points of view. This variety of viewpoints stimulates explanations and brainstorming remedies, implications, or modifications.

• An immediate debriefing with the users or developers is especially useful in generating modifications and even new ideas for the product.

• Training observers for what to look for is useful, especially when particular items are of major concern to the developers.

In addition, three cautions are important to consider:

• Observers need to be alert to unanticipated outcomes or events.

• While attending to specified concerns, observers need to note especially any potentially negative occurrences or results because those must be dealt with before implementing full-scale use of the product.

• Observers must be careful to record *what* they observe rather than their opinions or judgments or inferences. The latter are more usefully dealt with during the debriefing and analysis of the observation.

Interviews

Interviews are actually oral questionnaires. They are often used effectively to follow up written questionnaire responses, especially to clarify or elaborate promising responses, or those that may be incomplete, unclear, or confusing. Interviews can be tailored to specific respondents but must still meet the basic requirements of effective feedback questionnaires:

• Focus responses on specific components of the product being evaluated.

• Specify clearly the variables to be commented on.

• Require suggestions or reasons or some other elaboration by the respondents that will be helpful in dealing with any flaws, omissions, or suggestions noted.

Unlike questionnaires, actual interviews may alert evaluators to unanticipated concerns or problems simply through the nonverbal behaviors of the interviewees. Such behaviors can then be probed for explanations.

Interview protocols—the list of questions to be asked— must be constructed as carefully as questionnaires in terms of the sequence of questions, the structure of the questions, and the language used. Avoid prompting, or "telegraphing," desired responses or "loading" the results. Questions, for example, must not telegraph a preferred response, force convergent responses, assume anything at all, or provide answers to other later questions. A question that begins, "What problems did you have with X?" may force an interviewee to invent a problem simply to appease the interviewer. Questions that focus on only one part of a product or lesson may steer interviewees away from the parts they had problems with or have useful suggestions about.

Unstructured interviews may also prove useful in certain instances. One type of unstructured interview begins with the interviewer asking the interviewees simply to talk about the product they just used. The interviewer then probes for details and other specifics as the interviewees touch on points critical to the evaluation. What might begin as a free-wheeling, open-ended interview—starting perhaps with, "Well, what do you think?"—can thus quickly zero in on problem areas and suggestions for dealing with them.

Another type of unstructured interview is what Borg (1987) describes as having interviewees "talk" through the ideas that occurred to them as they used the product, participated in a specific educational activity or experience, or tried to apply in a new setting what they had learned through such an experience. In so doing, interviewees may bring up points or reveal problems or alternative ways of doing something completely unanticipated by the evaluators or developers.

Focus Groups

A focus group is nothing more than a group interview. It is usually directed by someone other than the developers or authors of the product—to ensure candid and uninhibited responses. A focus group concentrates on evaluating the product and, where possible, on generating remedies for any problems that the group identifies. The group can be homogeneous in composition. All novice users might constitute such a group, for example, or be subdivided into several focus groups to keep each group small enough so all members feel free to and will contribute as often—and in as much detail—as they feel moved to do.

The session can begin with general questions like these:

- What worked especially well?
- What gave you the most difficulty?
- What would you have it (the product) do differently?

After that opening, the focus group leader should probe for reasons and examples related to selected components and aspects of the product, zeroing in on the specifics. Then, the leader may ask individuals to attend, in turn, to those components or aspects of the product of particular concern to the developers.

Focus groups are useful because they allow an evaluator to get feedback from more than one person at a time. They also allow comments and ideas to build on each other—to contradict them, to add details, or to generate diverse remedies. And they help evaluators identify when a problem is common or widespread rather than idiosyncratic to a particular individual.

On the negative side, focus groups, unless deftly directed, can easily be dominated by one or two opinionated individuals. Leaders may also need to make special efforts to draw out reticent individuals or to probe for specific instances or examples in support of vague generalizations.

Video and Audio Taping

Taping a trial use of a product under development is not so much a method of gathering information as it is of simply recording an event for later interrogation and analysis. Recordings allow evaluators to examine the trial at their convenience and to review it as many times as they wish. Yet we must still do the work of gathering evaluative data from the recording, through observation or by analysis of transcripts. All the points about observing events, noted previously, also apply to recording events.

One important advantage of recording a product tryout for later analysis is that the key participants in the event can view or listen to the tape as it is replayed. This permits evaluators to stop the tape whenever they wish to seek explanations for participant actions or responses, to query them about perceived problems, and to solicit suggestions for modifying tasks or content that appear troublesome. To facilitate this type of information collection where classroom teaching is the subject of the evaluation, the use of two cameras and a split-screen image is useful, with one camera continuously focused on the teacher and the other on the class.

Computers can be programmed to record and track in the software management system the use of newly developed software and thus, in effect, provide records of a trial. Those records can then be analyzed in the same way as video or audio recordings to provide formative feedback. For instance, a system management component of a piece of software can record the following:

- The number and sequence of incorrect responses
- The time it takes for a user to respond to given tasks
- The time devoted to various parts of a program
- The number, kind, and sequence of erroneous responses to items in the software

All this information serves as useful feedback in revising software or other instructional material under development.

Anecdotal Records

Open-ended, free response—even stream of consciousness—records or notations made during or immediately after the using or testing of a newly developed product can also provide helpful information. One problem, however, is that the authors of such records may unintentionally fail to supply the kinds of information we need as developers. Yet such records can alert us to unanticipated aspects of our work, especially to unusual opportunities for enhancing its quality and to potentially significant negative aspects of the product.

Open-Ended Critiques or Reports

Open-ended critiques are exactly that—structured or unstructured, free-response evaluations that allow evaluators free reign in what they choose to focus on or write. These reports often serve as convenient vehicles for providing useful feedback. However, if we don't provide structure or prompts, the contents of such reports may not always provide the kinds of information we need to improve the product. Thus, open-ended assessments should be accompanied by a few prompts to focus the evaluators on the types of information required. Some useful general prompts include:

> • What are the strengths of this product as you see them?
> • What are the weaknesses?
> • What could be done to eliminate each of those weaknesses? Where?
> • What did this fail to include that you wished it had included? Why is this important to include?

Provide additional prompts, as appropriate for the product.

Guidelines for Planning a Formative Evaluation

We can also use other information-gathering instruments and procedures in the formative evaluation of educational products. But regardless of the procedures or instruments used, these guidelines should be followed:

• *Collect data at several points in the development process.* The major points for such evaluations are when:

– the design or platform of the product has been drawn up,

– prototypes of each component have been drafted,

– a limited number of intended users pilot the revised prototypes, and

– large numbers of a representative sample of intended users try out the product from start to finish in a real-world context.

When we conduct evaluations at each of these points, we can revise the product as it grows to more closely approximate the ideal model of the product or a more workable, practical version of what was originally proposed.

• *Use multiple data-collection methods at each point in the evaluation process.* Only when we use the results of different data-collection and analysis methods can we rise above the idiosyncracies of our respondents or ourselves—biases, prejudices, preferences, limited experience, and points of view—to justify revising a product under development. No single evaluation or procedure should be relied on to generate changes in a product.

• *Take the same care in developing evaluation instruments or procedures to be used for formative purposes as you do with the educational product itself.* Any questionnaire, interview protocol, procedure for generating annotations, or error log direction must itself go through a mini-development cycle and be evaluated formatively by experts, specialists, and a representative sample of the intended users *before* we use it to gather information.

To dash off and administer a formative evaluation instrument without submitting it to formative evaluation seriously undermines the validity of the instrument and the quality of the product that results from its use. The key to the recommended mini-development cycle of new instruments is to strike a balance between (1) no formative evaluation (including field testing) of new evaluation instruments and procedures and (2) expending endless time, effort, and funds on repeated cycles of revision and evaluation.

• *Do not confuse or equate formative evaluation with editing.* Many evaluators, unfortunately, approach formative evaluation as the latter and concentrate on spelling, colors, paragraphing, and the like. While such features of a product may need to be corrected, changes like these rarely address the issues of most concern to developers. Formative evaluation deals with the substantive more than with the cosmetic.

• *Based on the results of the formative evaluation, modify or revise the product at each point in the development process, before the next round of testing and evaluation.* It is hardly worth going through formative evaluation unless we are willing to make the revisions called for, even when the changes compromise or challenge our pet theories or "ideal world." Willingness to use the results of a formative evaluation to shape a final product and making serious efforts to do so distinguish quality development from superficial, backroom production of educational fads.

No matter what kinds of evaluation instruments and procedures devised or selected for formative feedback, we, as developers and evaluators, must remain constantly alert to two critical problems:

• *A tendency on the part of some evaluators to ask for, and for many respondents to provide, general or global judgments and comments.* The question "Were the objectives appropriate to the students' levels of ability?" or the response "The objectives were not relevant to my interests" exemplify such global statements. General questions or statements are useless because they fail to tie the responses to specific items or places in the product so those items can be revised, dropped, or otherwise improved. Unless evaluative prompts and responses are tied explicitly to specific items (as "to objectives 1, 2, and 3 in part I," for example), they will not generate revisions that will help improve the quality of the product.

• *The Hawthorne effect.* Many people selected to try out a new product are flattered by the attention given them and reciprocate with less than honest or candid feedback so as not to offend the individuals who chose them to participate in the first place. Evaluation instruments and procedures must be sensitive to responses that praise the product being assessed or that give feedback that the developers would *like* to hear—or that the respondents believe developers would like to hear, or because of the developers' prestige, certainly believe they deserve to hear. Such responses do not help improve the quality of a product. To minimize the Hawthorne effect, construct procedures and instruments as objectively as possible. Try not to identify any particular part of a product as the work of a specific individual, and use evaluators not associated with the developers.

* * *

The key to an effective formative evaluation is the kind of evaluation instruments and procedures used to elicit feedback. The techniques and guidelines—and cautions—described here can make a formative evaluation as productive as possible.

5
Formative Evaluation in Practice

HOW IS AN APPROPRIATE FORMATIVE EVALUATION OF ANY CURRICULUM or instructional development effort conducted in practice? This chapter provides examples of formative evaluations, ranging from large-scale programs to the design of a course for a local school district. These efforts illustrate many essential features of formative evaluation and the functions they serve in developing educational products.

Formative Evaluation in Large-Scale Development Projects____

A Multigrade Elementary School Curriculum

Robert Karplus (1975) directed the development of a major national elementary school science program (SCIS) from 1958 to 1977. The process of developing and evaluating the teaching kits, activities, and units employed by this project illustrates one way to carry out formative evaluation in the development of instructional products.

Besides obtaining feedback from the distinguished experts on his steering committee, Karplus involved all staff members in generating and critiquing ideas for learning activities and program materials. During the initial design of each of these products, he reported, "Elementary school teachers and sometimes secretaries on the project staff served as the first 'guinea pigs,' using the new activity after it had been worked out by its inventors, since their lack of scientific training made them the most naive subjects readily available to the project" (Karplus 1975, p. 76).

For this early feedback, a single individual usually executed a proposed activity under the observation of one or more of its developers. The team thus got an initial sense of the workability of the activity, as well as what needed to be done to ensure it would and could be used by its target audience as intended.

Once Karplus and his staff had materials or activities they believed would work, they then tried them out in actual classrooms:

> Classroom trials played an extremely important role in the work of the SCIS and were the ultimate way of acquiring the information on which final decisions regarding segments of the teaching program were based. . . . Development staff participated in these trials as much as possible.

Classroom trials took place in three stages. The first, called "exploratory teaching," occurred very soon after an activity had been invented and again when a unit was revised. It was carried out completely by project staff members functioning as "guest instructors" in elementary school classrooms. At least two, and sometimes four or five, members of the development staff planned and participated in exploratory teaching. They took the necessary equipment, pages of instructions for students, and sometimes video or audio recording equipment to the classroom. One of the staff members actually conducted the class, while the others observed the sessions, sometimes interviewing children who were experimenting individually concerning their ideas, questions, or intentions. After every exploratory session, one or more of the participating staff members prepared a written report in which the activity, the children's reactions, and the operation of the apparatus were described fully. These reports were filed and later served as raw material for the redesign of equipment, revision of the activity, and preparation of the teachers' guides and other publications. The activity was also discussed in a postmortem session in which every participant could express his or her views frankly.

The second stage of classroom trials was carried out by regular teachers in the three laboratory schools (one suburban, two middle-class urban) . . . in the Berkeley area after teachers' guides, student manuals, and apparatus kits for the teaching unit had been prepared by the project in the Trial Edition. These classes were visited regularly by the unit's developers and also by other staff members who observed the teaching, occasionally spoke to children if this did not interfere with the teacher's work, and conferred with the teacher concerning any questions the teacher might have. Reports of the observations were filed after the visits and ultimately served as source material for revision of the unit. Individual conferences, feedback meetings, and feedback questionnaires enabled teachers to communicate their reactions to the developers.

Regular teachers in the Berkeley area and in the five trial centers that had been established by the project in 1966 carried out the third stage of classroom trials. These teachers used the Preliminary Edition. . . . Project staff observed the classes in Berkeley, and local coordinators observed classes in the trial centers. Project staff also visited the trial centers, observed classes, and met with teachers two or three times a year. The coordinators submitted quarterly reports of their experiences in teacher education, classroom observations, suggestions from teachers, and specific comments concerning the teaching activities. All of this information was used in the preparation of the final edition of SCIS units, published by Rand McNally beginning in 1970. . . .

The design of the classroom trials involved setting up three feedback loops through which the project staff could test curriculum ideas on an ever-larger scale: first with one class of children or possibly 2, then with 10 classes and 10 teachers, and finally with 50 classes and 50 teachers in 5 different locations in the United States. The exploratory trials were used to test the children's reactions to proposed activities and equipment and to gather children's ideas to enrich the teaching activities. The Berkeley area trials were used to test the revised activities and to get a first response from teachers concerning the demands placed on them. . . . The country-wide trials, finally, sampled reactions from a larger number of teachers of very diverse backgrounds, with activities that were known to function reliably with children. (Karplus 1975, pp. 76–78)[3]

Karplus's delineation of the goals of this phase of formative evaluation are particularly instructive.

---

[3]Robert Karplus. "Strategies in Curriculum Development. The SCIS Project." In J. Schaffarzick and D.H. Hampson, eds. *Strategies for Curriculum Development*. Berkeley, Calif.: McCutchan Publishing Corp. 1975. pp. 76–78. Reprinted by permission.

These efforts led finally to national trials with large numbers of teachers and children. You can easily adapt these methods to the development of any kind of instructional procedures or materials, from a unit or course to an entire program in any subject or content area at any level and on any scale.

A Major Curriculum/Instructional Development Project

The experience of the national Biological Sciences Curriculum Study (BSCS) project of the 1960s illustrates another way to organize and secure formative evaluation:

> [During the actual development process, initial drafts of program materials] were circulated for comments among the writers for that version [of the program] as well as the other versions. They were then revised and recirculated for further comments until the final product met with the approval of the supervisor. . . . Writing teams held frequent meetings to plan and iron out conflicting views. (Grobman 1970, p. 9)[4]

Once the teams had prepared a draft of the materials—in this case, a text, lab manual, teaching guide, and teaching commentary—additional formative evaluation proceeded as follows:

> During the 1960–61 school year, some 115 teachers tried out the experimental materials in their classrooms with 13,000 students. These participating teachers were selected to represent geographic clusters in various parts of the country, with at least 6 teachers in each cluster. This was done to permit the experimental teachers to meet weekly in small groups to discuss their experiences and to send back reports to BSCS. All teachers using these materials had attended a 6-day briefing session in Boulder to prepare them for use of the materials. A further opportunity for orientation to the new materials was provided during the weekly meetings, since each was attended by a college biologist who had been a participant in the . . . writing conference, and who was prepared to answer questions concerning unfamiliar content or laboratory procedures.

---

[4]Hulda Grobman, *Developmental Curriculum Projects.* Itasca: F.E. Peacock Publisher, Inc. 1970. pp. 9–11. Reprinted by permission.

In addition to the weekly group reports, teachers sent back individual reports of their reactions and classroom experiences using the new materials. Each teacher's classrooms were visited by BSCS staff consultants at least twice during the year. And students were tested on newly developed objective-type tests to reflect the new content and skills of the experimental curriculum. At the same time, other types of reactions to the new materials were obtained. Professional societies in biology, education, and psychology, as well as a number of individual biologists and psychologists, were invited to review the materials and make suggestions. . . . Steering Committee members [also] visited experimental classrooms. (Grobman 1970, pp. 9–10)[5]

Following extensive revisions and additions, the project's materials were tried a second time the following year, on a much larger scale:

This tryout was by 350 teachers, all of whom had had some special training. Most attended a week-long briefing session in Boulder under BSCS auspices, but some had attended NSF summer institutes given by various colleges and universities independent of BSCS direction. . . . Again, data were gathered on the experience of the teachers and their 50,000 students. Additional reviews were obtained from experts. Feedback from these various sources were collated for use in the final writing conferences. (Grobman 1970, p. 11)[6]

Again, the teams revised the materials before publication and dissemination to schools. Additional materials designed to supplement these core materials were also tried out and evaluated in schools before being prepared in final form.

---

[5]Hulda Grobman, *Developmental Curriculum Projects.* Itasca: F.E. Peacock Publisher, Inc. 1970. pp. 9–10. Reprinted by permission.
[6]Hulda Grobman, *Developmental Curriculum Projects.* Itasca: F.E. Peacock Publisher, Inc. 1970. pp. 11. Reprinted by permission.

Development of a Textbook Series

Educational publishers have employed similar procedures in developing textbooks and other kinds of instructional materials. Science Research Associates (SRA), for example, undertook a 5-year project to develop a basal mathematics textbook series for elementary schools in the early 1970s. Besides seeking formative evaluation at the design and prototype-producing steps, this development effort included classroom tryouts and evaluation as well:

First drafts of chapters were prepared and carefully reviewed by authors, staff, and consultants. As a result of these reviews, chapters were revised and, if judged ready, prepared for classroom tryouts. . .

During the tryout year, the field observer made frequent visits to each of the classrooms in which the materials were being used. In-service training sessions were held at the request of the teachers. These meetings were usually conducted by the field observer and sometimes were attended by authors or members of the development staff. Teachers were also encouraged to telephone the field observer or the staff in SRA's Chicago office if they had questions.

Data were collected throughout the year. Valuable assessments of the material came through page-by- page reactions written by the teachers in their guides. Those pages were collected quarterly and consolidated for the review of authors and developmental staff who were already at work on revisions for the field verification study to be undertaken during the following year. Authors and members of the developmental staff also visited the sites to observe the children's use of the materials and to discuss with teachers the merits and the problems of the program. The field observers critiqued the texts page by page and submitted quarterly reports on their classroom observations. Standardized mathematics achievement tests were given in the 2nd through the 8th grades at the beginning and end of the year. Some comparisons between MLS and non-MLS classes were included in the data collection. The general reactions of teachers and of pupils contributed much to the final evaluation of the effectiveness of the materials. The most important information came from analyses of items on MLS chapter test results. Such analyses identified specific patterns of errors, which were extremely valuable in revising pages, adding or deleting materials, and improving instruction for the teacher.

The field verification study continued throughout the year, and data were collected from a variety of sources. Authors and developmental staff continued to play an important role in observing and reacting to the success of various components of the program. Comments from the hot line provided information about the kinds of help teachers needed in the implementation of MLS. Reactions of teachers and pupils were a constant source of important data for further refinements in the program. The sales staff's suggestions and reactions were carefully considered to ensure that the materials that were successful in the field verification study would be equally successful in the marketplace. Both pre- and post-achievement data were collected for approximately 1,500 learners at each level. (DeVault and Anglin 1975, pp. 173–176)[7]

As in other development efforts, the data collected during this stage of formative evaluation served as the basis for revisions, additions, and deletions in the materials before they were prepared in final form.

Formative Evaluation of Short Courses

In describing the development of new university minicourses, Borg and Gall (1989) cite three stages of field trial evaluations. The first, which they call a "preliminary field test," sought a qualitative evaluation of the proposed minicourse:

This evaluation was based primarily upon the feedback of a small group of teachers who take the course and the observations of laboratory personnel who coordinate the field test. As a rule, from four to eight teachers have been sufficient for the preliminary field test, since the emphasis of this evaluation is upon qualitative appraisal of course content rather than quantitative appraisal of course outcomes. . . .

---

[7]M. Vere DeVault and Leo Anglin, "Strategy for Curriculum Development: SRA Mathematics Learning System," in Jon Schaffarzick and David H. Hampson, eds. *Strategies for Curriculum Development.* Berkeley, Calif.: McCutchan Publishing Corp. 1975. pp. 173–176. Reprinted by permission.

Minicourse 1 was designed to be used by elementary school teachers during their regular school day. Therefore, the preliminary field test was carried out with six teachers from two elementary schools. Instead of this procedure, we might have invited the teachers and some of their students to our laboratory to take the course, perhaps on a speeded-up basis. The major problem with this procedure is that we might have obtained a very unrealistic impression of the course. Elements of the course that raise no problem in a laboratory setting might create havoc when used in the schools, causing an adverse effect on the course outcomes.

Throughout the preliminary field test of Minicourse 1, two field representatives . . . worked closely with the six teachers in order to obtain as much teacher feedback and observation data as possible. Each teacher was interviewed individually three times during the field test. These interviews focused upon specific problems and course deficiencies as well as suggestions for improvement. At the end of the course, each teacher completed a questionnaire regarding the course and participated in a group discussion with laboratory personnel. In addition to these formal contacts, each teacher had informal contacts with one of the [developer's] representatives each day. (Borg and Gall 1989, p. 790)[8]

After analyzing all the feedback data secured, the developers revised the course and then submitted it to a "main field test." They sought at this point to assess how well the new course met its performance objectives:

A single-group pre-post design . . . was used. . . . About 50 teachers participated. . . . Shortly before the course began each teacher was asked to conduct a 20-minute discussion in his or her regular classroom, and this discussion was videotaped. After the course was completed, each teacher again conducted a 20-minute videotaped discussion.

Each videotape was viewed by trained raters who made quantitative observations of teachers' use of the skills and behavior patterns presented in the minicourse.

---

[8]From *Educational Research: An Introduction,* fifth edition, by Walter R. Borg and Meredith D. Gall. Copyright © 1989 by Longman Publishers. Reprinted by permission.

As each videotape was coded and given to raters in random order, the raters did not know which were pretapes and which were posttapes. . . . Questionnaire and interview data should be obtained from all participants in the main field test. (Borg and Gall 1989, pp. 791–793)[9]

A third field test then occurred, this time of the complete minicourse without the presence of the developers. Borg and Gall refer to this stage of evaluation as an "operational field test":

The operational field test is set up and coordinated by regular school personnel and should closely approximate regular operational use. Feedback from both the coordinators and the teachers taking the course are collected by means of questionnaires. . . . The main use of these data is to determine whether the course package is complete. Interviewers focus on parts of the course that fail to do their job or on materials that are needed in order to make the operation of the course easier or more effective. (Borg and Gall 1989, p. 793)[10]

Formative Evaluation of Local and Small-Scale Development Projects

Schools and individual educators also engage in curriculum and instructional development, although obviously not on the scale of most development projects described here so far.

Development of a Middle School Sex Education Course

For example, in developing a sex education course for middle school students, one school district incorporated formative evaluation at the following points in the development process (Edgemon and Thomas 1979):

---

[9]From *Educational Research: An Introduction,* fifth edition, by Walter R. Borg and Meredith D. Gall. Copyright © 1989 by Longman Publishers. Reprinted by permission.

[10]From *Educational Research: An Introduction,* fifth edition, by Walter R. Borg and Meredith D. Gall. Copyright © 1989 by Longman Publishers. Reprinted by permission.

- Once a draft of an instructional overview of the proposed course was prepared, parents were invited to examine and provide feedback on the proposed plan.
- For each of five iterations of the program as it was drafted and revised, a program steering committee provided formative feedback. The committee consisted of representative parents, religious leaders, health and medical professionals, and an educator experienced in developing such programs in other school districts.
- After the completed program was taught on a trial basis to a limited number of students, the three tryout teachers and their students suggested revisions, and parents had an opportunity to evaluate the program.

After additional revisions and full-scale implementation of the complete program at all relevant grade levels, evaluation by participating teachers, students, and parents continued. The course was adjusted to iron out problems and reflect changing community interests and educational goals.

Development of a Textbook Prototype

Borg and Gall (1989) describe the development of a prototype of a new type of textbook as a doctoral dissertation project. In this project, the author secured formative feedback on the prototype materials, as follows:

- Upon completion of a draft of the materials, they were evaluated for accuracy by two subject-matter experts, for community acceptability by local leaders, for curriculum fit by a local school central office administrator, and for bias by experts in this field.
- After a small-scale tryout of the materials by two groups of 8 typical students each, students completed a domain-referenced achievement test and a specially developed attitude scale and were interviewed by the author. The two participating teachers also completed a special evaluation form.
- After revision based on that tryout, a main field test involving 5 teachers and 20 classes was conducted as a pre- and post-test group experiment using a domain-referenced achievement test, attitude scale, teacher questionnaire, and interviews.

Other formative feedback was apparently also solicited and provided at additional points in the preparation of the platform or blueprint of the dissertation project, as well.

Curriculum Development in Elementary School Art

In a two-year, university-based, curriculum development project in elementary school art education, staffed by eight doctoral students and directed by Elliot Eisner (1979) of Stanford University, formative feedback was secured at four points, at least, during the process:

• During the drafting of a unit's lessons and materials in a review or critique by all authors and staff

• After the revision of the unit based on that review, by four elementary school teachers reading the material for clarity, usefulness, relevance, and classroom workability

• In a preliminary classroom tryout of the revised materials conducted by the 4 teachers and observed by project staff (Walker 1975)

• At the conclusion of a main field test by 20 teachers in their classrooms, by assessing student artwork, interviewing the teachers, and analyzing teachers' written comments on the curriculum syllabus used

According to Eisner's summary of the project, each formative evaluation generated information from which later revisions were or could have been made.

The Practice of Formative Evaluation

As these summaries of formative evaluation efforts indicate, such evaluations may be conducted in many ways, using a variety of data-collecting procedures and instruments. The evaluation efforts described here do not by any means exhaust the possible ways of conducting formative evaluation. Nor do these summaries indicate all the places where such feedback was or could have been solicited. However, they provide insight about how this feedback was obtained in actual development efforts, especially during the crucial part of the process when a new educational product is actually being created.

All these development efforts employed formative evaluation at the various points in the development process described in Chapter 2. Although they varied in scale and subject, the procedures used, questions asked, and types of instruments used were remarkably similar. Moreover, the evaluations described here highlight the functions served by particular types of evaluation. Karplus's SCIS project, for example, used initial field trials to actually generate better, more useful activities than had been originally designed. He and his colleagues also used criticisms and ideas stimulated in these early trials to flesh out existing activities and as data from which teaching guides were written.

Other developers used these field trials primarily to confirm how well their initial ideas worked as intended and often discarded those that didn't. Actually, field trials can serve at least these two functions simultaneously—but each function shapes the types of feedback needed, questions asked, and most appropriate data-gathering instruments.

The experience of the BSCS project points up the value of and need for extensively training the participating teachers in the demands and techniques of an innovative curriculum, teaching methodology, or other type of product before any formal evaluation of its use. For a valid assessment to occur, users must understand and feel comfortable in using an innovation. Otherwise, the result simply documents the trials and tribulations encountered by those unfamiliar with carrying it out. Too many development efforts attempt to use *outcome evaluations* too soon in the development process and thus, in effect, actually turn up data about the lack of expertise demonstrated by the users rather than about the innovation itself. Extensive formative feedback like that used by SCIS and BSCS in their early trials, as well as training and repeated opportunities for experimenting users to get comfortable using the new product, must precede any effort at summative or outcome evaluation.

Karplus's SCIS project also demonstrates the value and role of the developers themselves' conducting and observing early tryouts of a new product. No one presumably knows better what the original intent of a product is than do they. Of course, uncritical commitment to the product can sometimes turn such initial trials into blind endorsements rather than opportunities to modify or tune-up an often ragged and flawed idea. However, the SCIS project highlights the value of trying out ideas on "naive" subjects in the early design stages simply to see if the task or subject can be handled as intended or is mechanically workable, before putting it to any trial with its intended users in group or classroom settings.

The SRA development effort also highlights the value of teacher annotations of materials and teaching instructions, as well as item analysis of content assessments as sources of data for further revision of materials rather than as quantified summative judgments about quality. Borg and Gall, as do other developers, stress the importance of, at some point, conducting field trials in the actual setting and under the conditions typical of the settings where the product is to be used—as opposed to doing so in contrived, artificial, or laboratory conditions. And virtually all these evaluation efforts stress the usefulness of observing and interviewing instructors and students who try out a curriculum or instructional innovation.

* * *

Perhaps what these examples of formative evaluation illustrate especially well is the importance of *continuing formative evaluation throughout the development process.* Note that the first concern of the developers was the workability and clarity of their product. After repeated revision of successive iterations of the products, the developers' concern gradually shifted to an examination of educational effects. Although the processes described in this chapter differed considerably in the scale of the evaluations and in the attention to securing feedback, all solicited feedback at similar points through a variety of methods and instruments. Taken together, these examples show how most of the evaluative procedures described in these pages can work in actual practice. By reference to these examples of formative evaluation, we can generate and clarify alternative approaches to executing this important component of educational product development.

6
Guidelines for Planning a Formative Evaluation

HOW CAN ALL THE SUGGESTIONS FOR CONDUCTING FORMATIVE evaluations presented in this book come together in our practice? How can we effectively secure the viewpoints of experts, representative target users, and other evaluators? How do we plan evaluation procedures and design assessment instruments for different stages of the development process to generate the kinds of feedback that will be most useful in producing the best product possible?

Planning Matrix

There are many ways to structure a formative evaluation. Perhaps the most useful is to conceptualize or plan it using a matrix like that in Figure 6.1 (see the next page). This matrix specifies the four major stages of formative evaluation and their relation to each other, as outlined in Chapter 2. Note that this matrix is an elaboration of the chart in Figure 2.1. Completing this matrix in detail can be a useful first step in planning the formative evaluation of any kind of educational product or innovation.

FIGURE 6.1
Formative Evaluation Planning Matrix

Stage	Evaluators			What We Want to Know at This Point	Evaluation Procedures
	Experts	Users	Others		
1. Design (Blueprint)					
2. Prototype					
3. Pilot					
4. Field Trials Menu					

Menus for Planning

Figures 6.2 through 6.5 (see pp. 74–77) summarize the purpose, kinds of evaluators, conditions, essential questions, procedures, and instruments that could be useful at each of the four major stages of the typical development process shown in Figure 6.1. Reference to these summaries will prove useful when planning each segment of a formative evaluation. Note, however, that the questions listed in each are not intended to be literally asked of evaluators. Rather, the instruments and procedures finally selected must elicit information that is most relevant to improving the quality of the product under development. Except for the entries under *Purpose*, the information in these summaries represents possibilities and options; some are more relevant than others to any specific type of product development evaluation. All the items included here may not be incorporated in any single formative evaluation plan. Instead, these summaries can serve as menus or shopping lists, not as all-inclusive, prescriptive specifications.

Obviously, more detail must be included in any formative evaluation than can be accommodated on a matrix of the size presented in Figure 6.1. We can use a larger version of the matrix, such as large sheets of poster paper, or a computerized form, in designing an actual evaluation. This allows room to add details as the plan is assessed and as the time for carrying out each stage approaches. Using the matrix in Figure 6.1 with reference to the menus in Figures 6.2–6.5 can help us lay out an effective, ongoing formative evaluation of any educational product during the time it is being developed.

FIGURE 6.2

Menu for a Formative Evaluation of a Design, Platform, or Blueprint for a New Educational Product

Purpose: To determine the validity and appropriateness of the principles and guidelines that the product will be built and of its proposed components and structure

Evaluators
- Recognized experts or specialists in the various features of the proposed product—e.g., in content and subject matter, teaching and learning strategies, cognition, nature of the intended users, and specialized areas of concern (multicultural education, assessment, etc.).
- Recognized leaders of the intended users of the product, e.g.:
  - qualified supervisors, coordinators or administrators
  - representatives of professional associations representing target users

Evaluation Conditions: At a convenient place for each evaluator, such as an office, conference room, or home office

What Developers Need to Find Out
1. Are the product's specifications, consistent with and validated by sufficient research, tested theory, and exemplary practice?
2. How likely is the proposed product to resolve the identified problem or to accomplish its specific objectives?
3. How likely is the product to be used as proposed by its intended (target) users?
4. How likely is the proposed product to work as designed?
5. What has been omitted that should be included for the product is to work and be used as intended?
6. How much congruence exists among the product's intended objectives; its design features; the identified needs, interests, and other characteristics of the target users; and features of its real-world, intended context?
7. How well does the proposed product fit the current conditions of the context where it's intended to be used?
8. How valid and relevant are the program's assumptions?
9. How well will this satisfy the legal or policy requirements regarding the area where it will be used?
10. How well can this fit and be integrated into the intended real-world context?
11. How sufficient, accurate, relevant, and sequenced for understanding is the content for mastery?
12. Are the learning activities and materials consistent with the specified objectives, appropriately sequenced, and appropriate to the intended users' abilities and previous knowledge?

Feedback-Generating Procedures and Instruments
- Annotated documents
- Questionnaires
- Interviews
- Focus groups
- Open-ended critiques

From Barry K. Beyer, *How to Conduct a Formative Evaluation* (Alexandria, Va.: Association for Supervision and Curriculum Development, 1995). Copyright © 1995 by Barry K. Beyer. Charts and figures may be reproduced for educational purposes only.

FIGURE 6.3

Menu for a Formative Evaluation of a Prototype or Early Draft of a New Educational Product

Purpose: To determine the likelihood that the product will work as intended when used by the target users

Evaluators
- Experts or specialists in content, learning and teaching strategies, cognition, and the nature of the intended users
- Representative users (one-on-one tryout)

Evaluation Conditions: In a setting controlled by and convenient for the developer, such as a conference room, work room, or media lab or office

What Developers Need to Find Out

1. What, if any, gaps or irrelevancies are present within the program?
2. Is there sufficient content or practice for mastery and understanding?
3. Is the content or material accurate?
4. Are the components, materials, and activities (tasks) sequenced for understanding or mastery?
5. Are there congruence and consistency within and across all components?
6. Are the target users likely to have the knowledge, skills, and experience prerequisite for successful use of the product?
7. How appropriate is the product to the interest, abilities, and knowledge levels of the intended users?
8. Are the tasks and procedures appropriate to their intended functions and to the users' ability levels, knowledge levels, and prior experience?
9. What unanticipated negative or other outcomes of this product did or are likely to occur?
10. Will it work—or is it likely to work—as intended? If not, why not?
11. In terms of form and structure, will it be readily reproducible at a reasonable cost (if appropriate)?
12. Does the product engage user interest?
13. How is the use of the product affected by user differences?
14. Are directions and tasks clear, easy to complete, and doable by the users?
15. Can the users carry out the tasks in the allotted time?
16. How well does the prototype enact the design (blueprint) specifications?

Feedback-Generating Procedures and Instruments

• Annotated documents	• Focus groups
• Questionnaires	• Video and audio taping
• Self-generated critiques	• Learner or error logs
• Observations	• Examination of learner-produced
• Interviews	projects and other products (papers, essays, etc.)

FIGURE 6.4

Menu for a Formative Evaluation of a Pilot Tryout of a New Educational Product

Purpose: To determine how well a product works as intended when used as directed by typical representatives of the range of intended users

Evaluators: Include both:
- Novice primary users representing the extremes as well as the average of the range of intended primary users
- Experienced and novice secondary users representing the extremes as well as the average of the range of intended secondary users

Evaluation Conditions: In a setting controlled by the developer but resembling the kind of setting where the product is intended for final use

What Developers Need to Find Out
1. What are the gaps, irrelevancies, insufficiencies, and unnecessary redundancies in the product content and tasks or activities?
2. Are there congruence and consistency between the intended objectives, content, tasks or activities, and assessment?
3. Are directions, instructions, explanations, examples, and other important features clear to the users?
4. Can they use the product successfully and without difficulty to accomplish its intended objectives?
5. Can the users complete the tasks or activities involved in using the product successfully within the allotted time?
6. How actively engaged are the users when using the product?
7. What unanticipated consequences—especially negative or unusual consequences—occur during or as a result of the use of this product?
8. What kinds of adaptations do users make in the course of using this product that make it work better for them?
9. How practical, convenient, and acceptable is using this product as intended for the users?
10. How well does the product fit the expectations, experiences, interests, and concerns of its intended users?

Feedback-Generating Procedures and Instruments

• Annotated materials	• Interviews
• Observations	• Video and audio taping
• Questionnaires	• Error logs
• Learning logs	• Anecdotal records
• Focus groups	• Examination of learner-produced products

FIGURE 6.5

Menu for a Formative Evaluation of a Large-Scale Field Trial of a Newly Developed Educational Product

Purposes
- To determine how well a newly developed product, when used by its intended users as directed in a real-world setting, enables users to attain the specified objectives
- To identify anything that is incomplete or too difficult for successful use of the product in a real-world setting

Evaluators: Significant numbers (from 50 to 500 or more) of a representative sample of intended, novice, primary, and secondary users (as appropriate)

Evaluation Conditions: Real-world setting where the product is intended to be used, such as classrooms, offices, or media centers

What Developers Need to Find Out
1. Can a representative sample of its intended users actually use the product as designed in a real-world setting?
2. How well are the objectives specified for the product achieved when used as directed by its intended users?
3. What, if any, are the negative consequences of its use?
4. What, if any, are the unanticipated consequences of its use?
5. When used as intended, how workable, convenient, and acceptable is the product for the users?
6. What do users need to know or be able to do better to use the product successfully?
7. Does the product work equally well with the range of users it was designed to accommodate?
8. What, if any, are the gaps, irrelevancies, insufficiencies, and unnecessary redundancies in the product content, tasks or activities, and structure?
9. How well does the product fit the expectations, experiences, interests, and concerns of its intended users?
10. In what ways could using the product be made easier?
11. What, if any, problems were encountered during the use of the product? How might they be overcome?
12. What, if any, components of the product did not accomplish their intended objectives or did not work as well as they could or should?
13. Can the product be used to the degree of thoroughness desired in the time allotted for its use?
14. What were the alterations in or deviations from the way the product was directed or designed to be used?

Feedback-Generating Procedures and Instruments
- Annotated documents
- Interviews
- Observations
- Learning logs
- Focus groups
- Error logs
- Anecdotal records
- Video and audio taping
- Quantitative performance and achievement data
- Examination of learner-produced products

Formative Evaluation—Some Guidelines

Formative evaluation, in sum, is an essential part of any educational product development effort, whether we are creating a complete curriculum or program, a module in a course, a textbook or other type of instructional material, a strategy or procedure for teaching, or an administrative procedure or structure. Its purpose is to ensure that the product being developed is likely to achieve the objectives set for it, if used by the target users as designed. Formative evaluation is an ongoing part of the development process. It involves assessing how well the product meets certain standards, criteria, or conditions and how well it achieves designated objectives. The results of formative evaluation become recommendations for revising the product. Without formative evaluation during the development of an educational product, product revision and improvement are impossible.

Conducting a formative evaluation of an educational product during development is obviously a task not to be lightly undertaken. But any such evaluation can be done well, if we follow these guidelines:

• Carefully plan the formative evaluation *before* the development process gets under way.

• Evaluate at several different points in the development process.

• Use multiple evaluation methods, procedures, and evaluators to collect formative feedback at each evaluation point.

• Validate the methods, procedures, and instruments to be used in the evaluation *before* they are used.

• Focus each stage of evaluation on securing the kinds of information that will be of immediate use in improving the quality of the product.

• Seek explanations for evaluative judgments and, wherever possible, specific suggestions for dealing constructively with criticisms or perceived weaknesses.

• Use the results of each evaluation to modify, revise, or otherwise shape the product as it moves through the development process.

• Allow enough time to develop evaluation instruments and procedures, to gather the evaluation data, and to process the data so you can revise the product before the next stage of development or formative evaluation.

All these suggestions are predicated on one assumption: that the product being evaluated is being used as designed while its use is being evaluated. This is a dangerous assumption, for in practice users do not always use an educational product as its developers intended. Therefore, an essential part of any formative evaluation involves ensuring that the product is indeed being "used as directed." Any deviation from the prescribed use or any introduction of extraneous materials or other factors must be noted and their impact made explicit in judging the quality or other traits of the product. While it may not be the role of the evaluator to ensure the integrity of the product through its trials, it is crucial that those in charge of the evaluation monitor its use to ensure that the product is consistently used as directed or, at least, to note carefully and make explicit deviations from what is intended. Only in this way will formative evaluation produce useful feedback.

*   *   *

The guidelines presented here obviously present a rather idealized description of formative evaluation and of some specific ways to conduct it. In practice, however, we often feel or are actually forced to compromise these ideals. The pressures and temptation to do so are great. Yet we (and our sponsors) need to be aware of the negative consequences of cutting corners in terms of resources, time, and effort devoted to formative evaluation, of numbers of evaluators or evaluation points, and of the kinds of depth of evaluative data sought. Ultimately, corner-cutting compromises the quality of the product. A less-than-thorough, less-than-adequate, less-than-systematic formative evaluation will almost certainly result in a less-than-adequate product. If we seek to produce the best possible products, we must conduct honest, thorough, well-executed formative evaluations. The principles and guidelines presented here will contribute immensely to the accomplishment of this goal.

References

Baker, E. (1973). "The Technology of Instructional Development." In *Second Handbook of Research on Teaching*, edited by R.M.W. Travers. Chicago: Rand McNally College Publishing Company, pp. 264–267, 270–273.

Borg, W.R. (1987). "The Educational R&D Process: Some Insights." *Journal of Experimental Education* 55, 4: 181–187.

Borg, W.R., and M.D. Gall. (1989). *Educational Research: An Introduction*. New York: Longman. 5th ed., pp. 764, 787–802.

DeVault, M.V., and L. Anglin. (1975). "Strategy for Curriculum Development: SRA Mathematics Learning System." In *Strategies for Curriculum Development*, edited by J. Schaffarzick and D.H. Hampson. Berkeley, Calif.: McCutchan, pp. 173–176.

Dick, W., and L. Carey. (1985). *The Systematic Design of Instruction*. Glenview, Ill.: Scott, Foresman. 2nd ed., pp. 203–206, 225–232.

Edgemon, A.W., and W.R. Thomas. (1979). "How We Improved Our Sex Education Program." *Education Leadership* 38, 4: 256–258.

Eisner, E.W. (1979). *The Educational Imagination*. New York: Macmillan, pp. 139–143.

Fenton, E. (n.d.). "Criteria for Judging Curricular Materials Before Classroom Trial." Unpublished manuscript, Carnegie-Mellon University.

Gagne, R.M., and L.J. Briggs. (1974). *Principles of Instructional Design*. New York: Holt, Rinehart and Winston.

Grobman, H. (1970). *Developmental Curriculum Projects*. Itasca, Ill.: Peacock.

Karplus, R. (1975). "Strategies in Curriculum Development: The SCIS Project." In *Strategies for Curriculum Development*, edited by J. Schaffarzick and D.H. Hampson. Berkeley, Calif.: McCutchan, pp. 76–78.

Lytle, J.S. (1991). "Professional Presentations: Design and Evaluation of an Oral Communication Skills Course." Unpublished doctoral dissertation, George Mason University.

Pratt, D. (1980). *Curriculum Design and Development*. New York: Harcourt Brace Jovanovich, pp. 228, 342–344.

Raths, J.D. (1971). "Teaching Without Specific Objectives: Twelve Value Components for Selection of Activities." *Educational Leadership* 27: 714–720.

Schaffarzick, J., and D.H. Hampson, eds. (1975). *Strategies for Curriculum Development.* Berkeley, Calif.: McCutchan.

Scriven , M. (1967). "The Methodology of Evaluation." In *Curriculum Evaluation,* edited by R.E. Stake. Chicago: Rand McNally.

Stenhouse, L. (1975/1988). *An Introduction to Curriculum Research and Development.* London: Heineman, pp. 104–105.

Taba, H. (1962). *Curriculum Development: Theory and Practice.* New York: Harcourt, Brace and World, pp. 316–343.

Task Force, National Council for the Social Studies (1993). *Curriculum Standards for the Social Studies.* Washington, D.C.: National Council for the Social Studies.

Walker, D. (1975). "Curriculum Development in an Art Project." In *Case Studies in Curriculum Change,* edited by W. Reid and D. Walker. London: Routledge and Kegan Paul, p. 95.